GW01402686

Acknowledgements

'Nightfall' appeared in Cambrensis magazine, was a finalist in the SAMWAW competition and runner up in the Chapter One competition and appeared in its anthology.

'Lagly' was a winner in the Swansea Grand Theatre competition, was broadcast on Swansea Sound and was runner up in the Bloomsbury Writers' and Artists' competition.

'Calling Back' was first broadcast on the BBC and published in Momentum, Executive Retirement and the Michael Terence Publishing anthology, being highly commended in their competition.

'What a Performance' was published by Peterloo Poets' magazine, Poetry Matters.

'Jangle Bells' was first published by Cambrensis, then soundwork-uk.co.uk.

'Recycled Waste' was published by Momentum.

'Assault and Bartery' was published in Window on Wales.

'Postscript' reached the Chapter One competition shortlist.

'Finisher' was a finalist in the Tees Valley Writers' competition.

'Joint Account' was a finalist in the Almond Press competition.

'Not Writing Exactly' first appeared in Planet magazine.

'Catchy Numbers' reached the shortlist of the Wrekin Writers' competition.

'Escalation' was published by Momentum and Window on Wales.

'Letter to the Editor' was published in Locks magazine.

'Beauty and the Beast' appeared in Window on Wales, and was a finalist in the SAMWAW competition.

'Loudmouth' was first published on the soundwork-uk.co.uk website.

'Stocktaking' was shortlisted in the Exeter Story competition and published by Fairlight Books (UK) and Eucalyptus Lit (USA).

'False Reports' was longlisted in Cinnamon Press's New Voices Award.

NEAL MASON

False
REPORTS

Michael Terence
Publishing

To R. H.

Contents

Lagly

It's thieves like him that give prisons a bad name! All the same, these amateurs. Make me sick. No pride in their work. Like everything nowadays; sloppy. No standards. Can you find a safe-cracker who knows his Chubb from his Yale? Ha! When *I* was young, he'd know to a milligram how much explosive to use. Nowadays, they slap it on like plastering a wall. Instead of blowing the lock, they blow up half the bank. Costs more in explosives than they get from the safe – or would do if the explosive wasn't kicked.

You've only got to look at him. A kid, that's all. They don't want to know about apprenticeships these days. Straight out and earn some money. You try to teach them, but it's no use. He could learn so much from an expert like me. First, he steals a getaway car. A Lada.

'Best car in the car park,' he said.

'What were the rest? Reliants?'

Anyway, having opened it with his lock-picking equipment – a four-pound lump hammer – he begins to wire up the ignition. An hour later, with half the wiring loom dismantled, he's managed to make the wipers and hazard lights work. You can imagine it – I wish *I* had. Wires everywhere. Car looking like a dishevelled hedgehog. These kids know nothing. They won't listen. Funny thing is, he's always got his nose in a book. How does he think I reached the top? Not by reading, that's for certain. I watched, I listened, I copied. It takes time – and a little more subtlety than a lump hammer. When *I* pull a job, Scotland Yard goes into a panic. I'm only inside because of bad luck.

He gets the car going, eventually. I was trusting enough to leave him to it. Should have known better. Simon's always been unreliable. Just like his Mother. She gave birth to him in Marks and Sparks. Wouldn't have mattered, but she was robbing the place at the time. She's a shoplifter, see. They could hardly get to the baby for all the nicked baby clothes under her coat.

Well, while Simon's pinching the car, I'm up to my neck in cold water. In a water tank in an attic. And where's the attic? On top of the Amman Gallery. Clever huh? I'd walked in as an ordinary, fee-paying visitor. Already recced the place, of course, like the thorough professional I am. The next bit took a matter of seconds; I climbed on a chair in an empty corridor, then disappeared through the attic hatch. But I'm smart, see – not like Simon, despite his reading; I realise the security guards might check the attic when the gallery closes. But they'd never think to look in the water tank. Especially as it's January and five degrees below freezing…

Simon doesn't really have the brain for crime, to be honest. He's not thick; he doesn't have the razor-sharp perception, the finesse. And kids won't be told.

So, there I am in the tank. It's not what you'd call pleasant, but determination marks out the men from the boys. I raise an arm to check my watch – being careful, of course, not to make any noise while cracking the surface ice. Only an hour to go…

I met his Mother at Pwllheli Butlins. She was a chamber maid. I was on a working holiday – 'holiday' in that I'd booked in as a resident; 'working' in that I was pillaging the place. Rifled chalets while holidaymakers were sunbathing or entering knobbly knees contests. That's how I met her; she caught me ransacking her room – and what a gold mine *that* was: jewellery, cameras, radios by the dozen. Could have been awkward, mind, but I got her talking. She was on holiday too. From shoplifting. She fell for me straight away, of course.

The hour in the tank passes very slowly. It's all I can do to climb out. I lurch towards the attic hatch but, with no feeling in my feet and legs, I step between the rafters. The plaster shatters like ice. Hurtling down, I admire a sunny landscape in oils. As I'm descending the stairwell, my appreciation of it's rather brief.

In crime, as in life, resilience is what counts. That's the difference between me and Simon, see. Just because I've fractured a leg and the burglar alarms are deafening and I'm purple with cold, it doesn't mean my plan's gone wrong. I'd known all along the alarms would sound the moment I appeared. It's simply a matter of time, of gathering masterpieces quickly.

Hopping as fast as possible, I climb the stairs. I make straight for a Cannelloni. I take out my penknife to cut the oil painting from its frame. I can't open the blade. It's not my numb fingers; it's obviously shoddy workmanship. Cheap, foreign junk. Should be banned! No standards. Throwing the useless penknife aside, I take the painting next to it, remove its glass and frame and hurry to the next masterpiece: a Tortellini.

Must hurry now. Stopping only to sneeze, I hop over to a priceless Tagliatelle. Frame off, glass off and tuck it under my arm. That's my lot. No sense in being greedy. What I've got must be worth thousands. That's the difference between a *real* professional and the others; knowing when to stop. All a matter of judgement.

The bout of sneezing's a problem. Not my fault, of course – just one of those things. It's a delay I could do without. Have *you* tried sneezing and hopping at the same time? Not possible. 'Once for a wish, twice for a kiss, three times for something better.' What do you get for twenty-five?

Finally, the sneezes stop and I bounce down the stairs feeling a bit like Zebedee. The alarms seem more urgent. I open the gallery door and there's our getaway car. The Lada. At least there are no police cars yet. Five hops and I'm in the car. Simon finds the ignition key, fastens his seat belt, adjusts the mirror, indicates to pull out and, at last, we're going. On three cylinders.

'Simon,' I say, 'I don't want to sound hypercritical, it being your first job an' that, but every alarm bell in the world's clanging. I didn't expect Formula One but, optimist that I am, I expected more than five miles an hour. And why are the wipers and hazard lights on? Could you manage just a fraction more speed? – or shall I get out and hop, and you can catch me up later?'

It isn't long before we hear police sirens. It's bad enough when the police give chase – on foot; it's worse when D.I. Fowler opens the door, a huge grin on his face.

'Hello Lagly. And where are *you* off to in such a rush?'

Humiliating. Degrading. A man in my position. A respected leader of the criminal fraternity. I'm unable to answer him – partly because I'm sneezing and shivering violently.

So here I am – all due to bad luck and Simon's incompetence. Not that *he* cares; all he does is lie on his bunk and read. It's all he ever wanted to do. Says I forced him to be my accomplice. His Mother agrees and blames *me* for the fiasco, would you believe? You do your best for someone, try to put them on the right lines, and this is what you get.

As an idea, the robbery was a work of art. As for the art itself, well, bad luck played a part there too. Couldn't take the paintings I'd intended. The paintings I took were watercolours. And, because I had hugged them close to me, and I'd taken them out of their frames, and my clothes were sopping wet…

But I'm too resilient to be disheartened for long. Lots of great men are like that. There's a big job I've got in mind. Very hush-hush, of course. Don't know much about it myself yet. All I'll say is it's in London this time. Kensington actually. The Something and Albert. It's a museum, you know. Now, when Simon and I get out, if I can train him in the use of explosives…

Calling Back

He stared at it for a long time, then propelled his wheelchair closer. It wasn't like the telephones he remembered from his youth; his parents' phone had been black, not green – but that was a quarter of a century ago in the sixties. And this one had push buttons instead of a dial.

He did a half-pirouette so that his left hand was close to it. Slowly, he reached out to touch the shiny plastic – at that moment it shrieked, as though awakened suddenly.

He withdrew his hand quickly. The noise surprised him, not only by its timing, but because it wasn't the ring of a bell; it was a high-pitched bleep. The engineer hadn't warned him. Gingerly, he reached for the handset and picked it up.

'Hello. This is Gareth Lewis speaking.'

'So is this,' came the reply. The voice was that of a young man. There was a pause. Gareth frowned.

'Perhaps you've dialled the wrong number,' he suggested. 'I've only just had this phone installed; it's a concession for disabled people. In fact, the engineer's still outside.'

'Oh, I'm sorry. I thought I'd dialled carefully. The trouble is, now I've pressed button A, I've lost my four pennies and I haven't got any more. Actually, I'm trying to phone for the local weather forecast.'

Gareth stared at the phone. He felt uncomfortable. The young man's voice was familiar; it was similar to his own voice, or a younger version of it.

'Excuse me,' he said cautiously, 'but did you say you put four pennies in the slot and then pushed button A? I may be getting old, but I'm certain those phone boxes were replaced years ago.'

'Surely not,' said the voice with a chuckle. 'All phone boxes are the same. I've yet to come across one that doesn't take fourpence. I'm sorry to have troubled you – as I said, I'm trying to get the weather forecast. I'm walking up the Black Mountain this afternoon; I just wanted to know what kind of weather I can expect.'

Gareth flinched. He was transported back to a day, twenty-five years before, when he'd been caught in a sudden storm.

'You're not going up there?' he asked with a chill in his voice.

'Yes, why not? I want to walk to the summit of Garreg Lwyd – it's hardly Everest!'

Gareth remembered how the sheep, like tiny clouds, had vanished into the rain. Foel Fraith had already been engulfed. The wind blew fiercely and raindrops stung his face. Within a minute or two the storm would be upon him.

'It's strange,' he said slowly, 'our names being the same. Excuse my asking, but… are you by any chance engaged to a girl called Iris? I know it sounds odd, but – '

'How do you know that? You must be clairvoyant! I was engaged to Iris only yesterday. Do I know you?'

Gareth picked his words carefully. 'Not exactly – but I've a strange feeling I know *you*.'

Although he was staring at his living-room wall, he could see the storm hurrying towards him. He had to find shelter quickly. Shielding his eyes, he tried to locate the triangulation point on the summit of Garreg Lwyd; he knew there was a makeshift shelter there – a rough igloo made of stones. He buttoned the top of his jacket and continued climbing.

'Perhaps you're acquainted with Iris,' said the young man. 'Is that how you know me? She meets a number of people through her work.'

Iris. Gareth reflected on the name. His eyes were drawn to the sideboard where, at one end, a black and white photograph smiled at him. The smile was as constant as the twenty-five years it had been standing there. Now, for the first time, it seemed to mock him.

'Iris', he said slowly. 'Yes, I knew Iris.'

'Knew? I don't understand.'

Gareth wheeled his chair closer to the phone. 'Will you answer a question?' he asked. 'So that we can be certain?'

The young man hesitated. 'What is it?'

'When you were engaged… when you asked Iris to marry you, she had a telephone directory in her hands, didn't she? She didn't answer at first; she put the directory onto a chair, smiled at you and said, 'That wasn't the connection I expected.' Then she put her arms round you and said, 'Yes, yes, yes!' Am I right?'

The shock at the other end of the line was audible.

Gareth continued. 'You work in the local surveyor's office and she works in Swansea. For Barclay's Bank.'

Faint clicks mingled with the rustle of electricity on the line. Gareth eased his position in the wheelchair and waited.

'Did *she* tell you all this?' asked the voice, exasperated. 'Who *are* you?'

Gareth realised that there was a strange silence outside the bungalow. The road seemed untypically quiet; no children, no footsteps and, most unusually, no cars, their drivers changing gear as they accelerated out of the bend.

'Listen to me,' Gareth urged. 'Listen. Don't go up Garreg Lwyd today. You mustn't go up Garreg Lwyd today!'

'Why on earth not? What's going on?'

'Listen. A storm could catch you unawares – as it did me. I could hear the trickle of a stream to my right, but then all I heard was the rain. It lashed down and the ground was boggy – my feet sank into it. I tried moving to the right, but the water was even deeper there. I struggled to the left and found solid ground again. By now I was soaking wet. I cracked my shin against a boulder. My only sense of direction was the slope. I staggered on, determined to find the shelter.' He paused, then said carefully, 'We're the same person – do you understand? You're me – and I'm you, twenty-five years on!'

'Don't be ridiculous!' But in the silence that followed, Gareth could almost hear the younger man thinking.

'Tell me your sister's name,' said Gareth. 'Not the one she's usually known by, but the private one you used to have for her.'

'Now you're assuming I have a sister.'

'Judith – that's her secret name, isn't it?'

Gareth's gaze went to the far end of the sideboard where another photograph watched him. She looked serious, her characteristic introspection caught for ever – the same look she'd maintained until the day she died. The relentless disease hadn't been able to impair her stoicism. But Gareth didn't speak of this.

'That day – that day on the mountain twenty-five years ago,' he urged, 'it's waiting for you. That day is today. The storm – it's gathering up there now. As I staggered through it, leaned against it, the ground suddenly levelled. I was shivering with cold. The visibility was down to a few feet. I decided to keep going straight ahead. Step after step I moved forward. Then I stepped into space! There was nothing there! I was falling – falling!'

Gareth went quiet. The phone felt sticky in his hand. He took a handkerchief from his pocket and wiped his face. Eventually, the voice at the other end spoke.

'Is that why you're disabled?' it asked shakily. 'Because of the fall?'

For some reason, Gareth wanted to resist answering. The truth, even put politely, sounded harsh. But his answer sounded even harsher.

'Iris left me,' he said, staring at her photograph. 'Not immediately, of course; she visited me for a long time – even after she got engaged to someone else. She married him about a year after my accident. I never saw her again.'

The younger man grew more agitated. 'This can't be happening. The things you're saying – I'm a sensible, averagely-intelligent man – I phoned for a weather forecast, but you, claiming to be me, you tell me my future, tell me private details you've no right to know!'

'Listen,' said Gareth quietly. 'When I came round, one of my eyes wouldn't open. There was a deep gash on my head, blood pouring from it. But the rain had stopped; the sun was shining again. I was in a pool of water a few inches deep – at the bottom of the old quarry. That's where *you'll* be lying this afternoon if you don't listen to me – at the bottom of Garreg Lwyd quarry with your back broken. And when you're almost dead, someone will find you – just in time.'

Still no sound came from outside; not even the call of a bird broke the silence. Gareth's eyes ran over the familiar items of furniture; the single chair specially designed for him, the pile of half-read newspapers, the dusty surfaces conspicuously lacking in ornaments.

'Look,' reasoned the younger man, 'I admit you've been uncannily accurate in everything you've told me, but do you honestly expect me to believe I've telephoned myself? And even if what you say is true, how on earth can it change anything? Forgive me, but you're crippled; nothing I do or don't do can alter that.'

'But how do you know?' Gareth tried to remain calm. 'Perhaps it's all been a horrible nightmare – you can stop it coming true. Save me from it! Don't go up the mountain. Everything will be different – you won't have to sit in this wheelchair for the next twenty-five years! Can you imagine that? Think how much you enjoy your work, how bright the future seems – think what it's like sitting here year after year. All for the sake of an afternoon on a mountain. Think of it, man!'

The two faces on the sideboard watched, one serious, the other smiling. Gareth gripped the handset as though it were a lifeline. It crackled in his ear. But his caller had made a decision.

'I'm sorry; I'm going to ring off.'

'No! You mustn't!'

'I must. I don't want you to think I've no sympathy for you – I have. I'm sorry for what you've had to go through, but I think you're confused. That's it, you're confused. I don't know how this conversation has happened, nor how you know so many things about me. But it can't go on – you hear me? It can't go on!'

'Wait!' Gareth wheeled his chair angrily. 'Don't let it happen!'

'Listen,' said the younger man. 'I'm going to climb Garreg Lwyd this afternoon and what you've described won't happen. It can't. I'm going to climb to the top and take in the view. Then I'll go back to the car, drive to Swansea and take Iris out for a meal. *That's* what will happen.'

'No!' cried Gareth. 'You mustn't!'

With a click, the phone went dead.

'Wait!' shouted Gareth. 'Wait!' But he knew it was too late. Nothing would be changed.

He sat there motionless.

The telephone engineer tapped politely on the door, then entered. He was embarrassed, but covered his awkwardness with a cheery smile.

'Sorry to disturb you, Guv. I've finished outside; only a little job to do in here and I'll be finished.'

Gareth heard a car pass by outside and a group of children chanted a ritual game. The engineer picked up a loose wire from the floor; the wire led to the back of the phone.

'As soon as I fix this wire to the junction box, you'll be connected. Shan't be in your way for more than a couple of minutes. After that, you'll be able to call anyone you want. Anyone at all.'

What a Performance

My dearest Mathilde,

Mein got, it was awful! Humiliating! I hate Paris! I hate the world! It doesn't deserve me. Oh Mathilde, if only I had your soft shoulder to cry on. Why are people so slow to recognise genius? Sometimes I wonder why I bother. It seems only you and I appreciate how wonderful I am.

This was to be my big breakthrough, the moment when Richard Wagner's name burst on Paris. Imagine; the Emperor commanding a performance of 'Tannhäuser' – and at the Paris Opera. Now I'd show them! No expense was to be spared. I'd have the resources of the leading opera house in the world. Fully aware of the quality of my work, I knew I couldn't fail.

Then a problem cropped up. The articles of the Paris Opera state that no composer may conduct his own work.

'Why?' you might ask.

'Why?' I asked.

It's a rule. You can rope in a complete stranger, you can put a monkey in evening dress and give it a baton or you can be given a conductor called Dietsch, who doesn't know a crochet from a crutch. I got Dietsch.

Ach well, I thought; there's always a snag. If I stand over him and kick him often enough, perhaps we'll manage. Then someone happened to ask who was doing the translation.

'What translation?' you might ask.

'What translation?' I asked.

Foreign works have to be sung in French, I was informed. 'But I'm German,' I argued. 'I think in German, I compose in German, Tannhäuser is a German minstrel-knight; the whole bloody concept is German!'

'Sorry,' they said. 'It's a rule.'

I kept calm. I didn't get upset. A translator was found – one Edmond Roche, a customs officer. An excellent fellow, I said. Excellent. But I felt obliged to point out – I hope they didn't think I was quibbling – that he didn't speak German. Nothing daunted, they found me one Rudolf Lindau to assist – a German, thank God. I was relieved. Until, that is, I realised he didn't speak French…

They say I have a bad temper. My dear Mathilde, you know very well this is not true; I have a *foul* temper! Is it any wonder? Under these conditions, *insanity* would be restraint.

But I regained my composure. We developed a working relationship. Doing without sleep and food, and economising on pleasantries, I shouted the libretto into shape. Finally, exhausted, relieved, I handed the text to the Director of the Opera. Who rejected it.

With remarkable self-control which frightened even me, I enquired whether Monsieur le Director of the Paris Opera would kindly indicate, if he wasn't too busy with artistic duties with one of the chorus girls, what exactly was amiss with the libretto. 'It doesn't rhyme,' he said. 'Libretti for the Paris Opera have to rhyme. It's a rule.'

It might not surprise you to learn, dearest Mathilde, that my health hasn't been all it should be of late. This, indirectly, hasn't had a beneficial effect on my furniture – particularly my carpets, the foam and teeth-marks doing nothing to improve the pile.

I consulted a doctor who, commenting on the fine condition of my teeth and gums, prescribed a diet of beefsteak for mornings and Bavarian beer for evenings. With the minor omission of the beefsteak, I adhered to his diet.

I pulled through. My health and spirits revived markedly when the French, rhyming 'Tannhäuser' went smoothly into rehearsal. At last, things were progressing and the singers and orchestra could get on with learning their parts and the scene-painters could finish the flats and the costume designers could fashion the dresses and I could get on with writing the ballet.

'What ballet?' you might ask.

'*WHAT* F---ING BALLET?' I enquired politely, tearing up three rows of seats and reaching for another barrel of Bavarian beer. I was in danger of losing my temper.

Mathilde, whatever else I am, you know I'm not a liar. Difficult to believe though it is, every work performed at the Paris Opera must have a ballet in the second act. You guessed it; it's a rule.

Mein Gott, I thought we Germans were rule-fixated; we've been merely dabbling! Let me explain. The art-loving, aristocratic, Second Empire audience – who were opposed to my work from the start – are in the habit of indulging in a riotous night on the town before deigning to saunter along to the theatre. They turn up, unless they're late, after the first act, just in time to appreciate their mistresses and bedfellows exposing themselves in what, with remarkable restraint, I shall call dancing. And I, the great – or would-be great – Richard Wagner was expected to provide the background noise. I refused. Standing by the string section, perfectly composed, I refused.

During the following weeks – while they were repairing the string section – I thought the matter over. And, with characteristic genius, I decided to turn the problem to my advantage. I wrote the Venusberg music. I gave it to the ballet master. Displaying good humour – I admit I'm not noted for my humour – I suggested we might find room for jugglers and can-can dancers. The idea seemed to upset his artistic sensibilities; how on earth could we find can-can dancers at such short notice, he scoffed.

My health deteriorated rapidly. Rehearsals continued, but without me. There were rumours I was dead. They may have been right. The Music of the Future was looking moribund too. 'Tannhäuser' had one hundred and sixty-four rehearsals. One hundred and sixty-four. More than enough to ensure competence, you might think. Painful though it is to relate, I suppose I'd better refer to the conduct of Albert Niemann, the lead singer.

Niemann is, let's say, an egoist – and if *I* say he's an egoist, it must be true. But at least I have something to be egoistic about. That lame-brained representative of cretin-culture decided my directions didn't match up to his own concepts of performance, so he introduced arch asides and vulgar gestures to titillate the audience. They, at each of the three performances, wildly applauded his antics – in the sections, that is, where they weren't blowing metal whistles at pre-arranged signals. The presence of Louis Napoleon notwithstanding, they disrupted the entire proceedings and made it clear what they thought of my revolutionary politics and my music.

Oh Mathilde, what a shambles. What a mess. It cost two hundred and fifty thousand francs of public money. Of that, Niemann was given fifty-four thousand francs and I received seven hundred and fifty francs. I gave my share to Roche, my mono-lingual translator.

It's almost perverse to mention it, but 'Tannhäuser' was a box-office success, although the takings were peanuts compared to the costs. It took, from those who came without metal whistles, record receipts. It took, from me, at least a hundred years of life. While we're on the subject of money, dearest Mathilde, can you lend me some? I'm financially ruined – artistically ruined too perhaps. I'm nearly forty-eight, for God's sake. If I don't hurry up, my Music of the Future will be a dream of the past.

Will you marry me? No, I suppose not; muses never marry artists – especially if they're broke. It's a rule. Besides, my wife wouldn't like it. Actually, she probably wouldn't care, so long as she was provided for. I love you, Mathilde. I just wish your surname wasn't Wesendonk. How's it going to sound to my admirers, if I have any, a hundred years hence? 'Have you heard the hauntingly poetic

'Wesendonk Lieder'?' It lacks a certain something. Perhaps I'm fated to failure and ridicule.

Well, dearest muse, it's late and I must open another barrel of beer. I'm thinking of composing a series of music dramas based on Norse mythology, but it probably won't come to much. I should have become a silk merchant like your husband. In fact, I should have become almost anything at all but a composer.

Your distraught, loving, insolvent,

Richard.

(Author's note: Although this letter is clearly fiction, it may frighten the reader to learn that its main facts are true, right down to the diet of beefsteak and beer. Nor did such ludicrous precepts of art die out in 1861.)

Rescue

The swell barged the lifeboat aside again. Another flake of paint loosened and flapped, hanging on for life. A grey seagull detached itself from a cloud, circled the boat, then sheered off as though alarmed. Giving up, the flake of paint let go, slid down a wave and disappeared in the evening light.

In a secluded cove, a boy looked out to sea, then closed his eyes. He stretched his arms wide as though welcoming the sea and the freshening breeze. When he opened his eyes, the yellow beach curved from his hands to his shoulders. On his left index finger stood a ruined lighthouse; the cliff path ascended from his right elbow. He knew it was high time to take that path. It was always time to go back.

Something caught his eye – something white, half-seen, that bobbed into sight, then disappeared. He stared out to sea. Studying the dim horizon, it crossed his mind his gaze was at a tangent to the world, as usual. But there was something out there all right. Above him, a cloud began flaking, pieces of grey falling seawards.

He checked his watch, its liquid crystal digits nagging his conscience. The strap was split and needed replacing. Moving to the water's edge, he shielded his eyes as though from sunshine and tried to focus on the distant object. Water hissed as storm clouds rearranged themselves. There was no doubt now; it was a small boat.

He was in trouble again, he knew. The school bus couldn't leave without him – he wished it would – and they'd mount a search. Familiar fears gripped his stomach and sharpened his senses. The boat was mastless and no oars were visible. He could make out curves of rope on its side. It was definitely a lifeboat.

The sky grew darker. The lifeboat drifted nearer, but no human shape was discernible above the curve from prow to stern. No-one seemed to be steering; waves nudged it this way and that.

He thought he heard voices. They got lost in the wind as the world blurred and rain began to fall. He made a decision. He took off his blazer and tie, his shoes and socks, then waded in. The water felt cold as it seethed round his ankles. By the time it was above his knees, heavy rain dotted the sea. The boat looked a long way away.

The voices were calling his name. They came from the cliff path, now lost in rain. He edged further out, drew breath sharply as a wave soaked him to the waist. The voices sounded nearer. A surge of fear coincided with a large wave; it lifted him by his armpits, his feet leaving the bottom. Instead of struggling back towards the shore, he began to swim towards the boat.

Terror soon threatened to overwhelm him. He couldn't see the boat; there was no way of telling whether he was on course. He considered turning back, but sensed the angry, waiting voices. Another voice, an inner voice, warned him he was swimming out to sea. He struggled on, swallowed water, his fear picturing his exhausted figure too far from shore, great waves shrugging off his tiny strokes. At that moment his right hand hit something solid. He fumbled, found a curve of rope and gripped it tightly.

It took a few minutes for him to regain his breath and his strength. The rain fell lighter now, but it was almost dark and a mist hung over the water. What, or who, he wondered, would be in the lifeboat? As he was about to haul himself up, he noticed lettering along the side. Hand over hand, he pulled himself towards the prow and read a ship's name: Orion.

The boat dipped sideways as he pulled himself in. He found himself on one of the wooden planks that served for seats. Quickly he glanced fore and aft. The lifeboat was empty. As though by sudden permission, he began to shiver uncontrollably. Water ran from his clothes. He peered shorewards. A dark smudge suggested land was there, but it was more distant than he'd expected. Straining to listen through the wind, he couldn't hear any voices.

The world became a vast and lonely place. He raised his arm to see the time, but his watch had gone. It was almost dark now. Unsteadily, he moved towards the stern. He found a tarpaulin tucked under a seat. Tugging at the tarpaulin, he managed to free it; it was heavy and of poor quality. Underneath it though, he found a wooden box.

He undid the old-fashioned clasps and raised the lid. The hinges resisted at first, then gave. He found himself staring at a gun. He quickly realised what it was. Memories of old films seeped back; the fat barrel, the cartridges like small cans of Coke. It was a Faerie pistol; the cartridges were flares.

He closed the lid. The rain had stopped and the sea felt, not angry, but merely irritable. Night isolated the boat, but he could see a few stars, although no moon. He decided to take off his wet clothes and cover himself with the tarpaulin. First, he felt his way to where the tiller should be. His hands explored what his eyes could hardly discern. He found a rough edge of wood and his heart sank; it was clear the tiller had broken off near the rudder. Moving forward, peering and feeling, his search confirmed what he'd suspected; there were no oars, no mast and no way of improvising them. He looked up at the few visible stars. Even if he had the means to steer, it would be little use; he'd never been taught to navigate by the stars. They twinkled their valuable information but, to him, it was all in code.

His shivering increased. He crawled under the tarpaulin and curled up. Fatigue and sleep vied with discomfort. He lost consciousness. He dreamed he was back at school, a place with children, but no parents. He'd hated the place at first; but he'd realised, gradually, that he preferred being without his parents. Often in trouble and punished, he managed as best he could. He seemed to be floating above the school, then inside it, yet still separate. The place appeared to be lurching.

He started, clutching at his bedclothes. His hands held the tarpaulin. Water leapt into the lifeboat. It twisted violently as a storm hurled it about and the wind cut tops off waves. He couldn't think. Fear and cold gripped him. Some things registered though; his clothes, which he'd spread out to dry, were gone. Water in the bottom of the boat ran this way and that, as though in panic. The darkness became phosphorescent.

Then, as though independent, his right arm reached out and found the box. His hand struggled with the clasps and lifted the lid. Clutching the butt, he drew the pistol towards him and opened it. He reached out again and his fingers found a cartridge. Raising the loaded pistol into the storm, he squeezed the trigger tightly.

The explosion jerked his arm, but the noise was snatched away. After a pause, a portion of cloud glowed red. It bled, as though wounded.

Retaliation was instant; a wave boarded and thrust his head against wood. Dazed, semi-conscious, he tried to rise, but fell back. He lay in the bottom of the boat, water rushing over him. Each breath was salt and foam. His coughs merely emptied his lungs of remaining air. They began to burn, sucking desperately. He couldn't raise his head. Immobile, paralysed by fear and weakness, he sensed a lightness, a giving in.

A pair of hands – they felt huge – scooped him up. He felt them dig under his shoulders and knees, then everything went dark.

When he regained consciousness, words were drifting around him. The voices came from the other side of a louvre door. From his position in a bunk, all that was certain was that he was on a ship. Sunshine glowed through the portholes.

'Concussion and exposure,' said one of the voices. 'Nothing food and sleep won't cure.'

'It's remarkable. Eight days at sea.'

'Nine. The Orion went down on December the twenty-third.'

'It's certain there are no other survivors?'

'Everyone else lost – including the boy's parents.'

'Not a happy start to his New Year. Let's hope nineteen hundred and six treats him a great deal better.'

Outside the portholes, smoke from the funnels made the sunshine hazy. The boy lay still, closed his eyes and said nothing.

Jangle Bells

Dear Andy,

Thank you for your letter. It arrived here at the North Pole yesterday, along with millions of others. Ho, ho, ho. What a sweet little boy you sound. There's nothing I love more than millions of letters the day before Christmas Eve; they keep me occupied in between packing presents, supervising the dwarfs, writing cards and loading sleighs and they help maintain my jolly, round-faced, good-humoured disposition (look it up in the old-fashioned dictionary I'm wrapping for you) Ho, ho, ho.

Yes, Rudolf's very well, thank you, and no, what you mention doesn't land in the sleigh when we're travelling at speed. Look him up in the old-fashioned encyclopaedia I'm sending you (instead of the multi-launch, zap-all infantry fryer – whatever that is) and you'll find him under ruminant quadrupeds with deciduous branching horns. Ho, ho, ho.

As for the leather and plastic devices you asked for, sweet child, I think perhaps you should refrain from searching Mummy and Daddy's bedroom and their magazines, very fine though your tracing is. I'm pleased last year's coloured pencils are proving so useful. Unfortunately, I feel you're not quite old enough to enjoy edible panties; they're similar, it's true, to lollipops, but your parents would no doubt confiscate them for their own use. Which reminds me; my name is actually St. Nicholas and is spelt rather differently from an undergarment. Perhaps you were thinking of St. Michael. Ho, ho, ho.

There was absolutely no need for you to worry that your letter and home-made envelope might not arrive, despite its crayoned stamp. The Post Office and I have an arrangement. You can't imagine their delight at being inundated with virtually illegible, misspelt demands for toys. Beaming with Christmas spirit which is uplifting to behold, they load all their sacks onto aeroplanes, fly them here to the North Pole and, with a cheery wave, drop them on me from a great height. I love it. It's all part of the tradition. It doesn't annoy me at all. It makes me shake with happiness. It's very cold up here. It's so cold I occasionally resort to a warming, seasonal toddy (toddy, not teddy – look it up).

Who are 'The Dingbats'? I've never heard of them. But I suppose I'm just an old fuddy-duddy and, just because their latest hit, 'Screwing You Is Like A Nuclear Holocaust', hasn't reached the Arctic yet and, by comparison, acid rain seems like manna from heaven, it doesn't mean I shan't distribute copies as fast as humanly possible.

Remember to be a good boy tonight. Pray for Mummy and Daddy and, judging by your letter, all your so-called uncles and aunts. And don't forget to pray for Mr. Stamp next door who, God help him, works for the Post Office. No, of course I shan't forget your pet spider's present. I've had nothing else on my mind for ages. You're wrong to suggest, just because I've got to visit every child in the world in the space of two hours, I'd overlook your pet spider. I love spiders. I adore them. Of course I do. I see them all the time. They crawl all over me. The North Pole's infested with spiders. They don't bother me at all really. I only tremble because it's chilly. I've got a cold. It's nothing. I love colds. They're wonderful.

Actually, I've been feeling a bit depressed recently. It's nothing to worry about. A few more glasses of Christmas cheer, which I've been taking since July, and I'll be fine. I hope you can read my shaky writing. By comparison, it makes you a calligrapher (look it up – ask Daddy to help you, if he's not too tied up. Ho, ho, ho.). It's the dwarfs. They're on strike for more money again. It's no problem. I can handle it. I love it. The satisfaction of a job well done. All by myself. It's wonderful. I'm so happy. They say they want bonus payments because of the population explosion. I don't care. Not really. I don't see what they've got to complain about. Where else could they find work up here? They earn a fair wage.

All they do is whinge. Same as the fairies. Don't talk to me about fairies. They prance about in their tutus, flashing their arses at all and sundry, and each one thinks she's modesty personified, whereas I know the satisfaction they get from being lashed to prickly Christmas trees. Sod the lot of them.

Has your house got a chimney? If not, don't worry about it. I don't worry about it. I don't worry about anything. Not any more. Don't forget to hang up your stocking. More importantly, don't forget to leave Santa a little drinky. Or a big drinky. Brandy. Scotch. Anything.

Well Andy, I must go now. Time to jump into the sleigh. Judging by his nose, Rudolf's tanked up as usual. Nought to sixty in three seconds. Ho, ho, ho. And yes, I assure you my long, snowy white beard is genuine. All too genuine. I was a young man last year when I took on this job. Now look at me. But I enjoy it. It's marvellous. I wouldn't swop it for anything. Much. Can you imagine the satisfaction I get from seeing tiny, innocent, sleeping faces like yours? Think how I feel at the prospect of all those Christmas-morning faces twisted with greed, their owners tearing paper off presents and throwing aside books and clothes as they search for cash. It's wonderful. I love it. You mustn't think, just because my helpmates in department stores are incompetent, condescending grumblies who behave like out-of-work actors, and that one of them refused you a snort of his snifta (whatever that is) that I won't make all your dreams come true. The way I feel at the moment, I could magic anything. It's wonderful. It's lovely. It's brandy.

My cold's getting better. I feel as though I've taken off. Tonight, you'll see me, beard a jet trail, speeding through your dreams. I'll feel young again, trouble far below. I'll leave behind all that pantomime about goodwill and wonderland. Who needs it? Not me. I've had enough of it. Besides, few people believe in me any more. I'm like a hangover from a Victorian party, the discarded wrappings of a bygone age. I don't care. Why should I mind? I feel happy. Who cares anyway? You do.

Yes, that's true. You do. That's sobering. You care. If I get pie-eyed and speed off into the ether with all the presents, you'll care. Well, it's not exactly love and goodwill to all men, but it's nice to think I'd be missed. It's delinquent tots like you who keep inebriate old farts like me sane. I suppose that means I've got to pull myself together. Red nose to the grindstone and keep smiling. Ho, ho, ho. You and your illiterate letters. When I was your age, I too thought the future was beaming. You think it's all going to be wonderful, don't you? The coming years are loaded with presents, aren't they? Well maybe. I hope so. Yes, of course they are. You won't be disappointed. The future's wonderful. You'll love it. It's lovely. I pray so.

But now I really must get on. I feel a bit better now. Merry Christmas. And don't discard those books – if only because I spent ages wrapping the bloody things.

Have a gloriously happy day. Your tired but ever-reliable,

Santa.

Recycled Waste

It was sunset as he reached the rubbish dump, a vast litter of colours beneath an orange-peel sky. Had anyone watched him enter, a greasy tramp with matted hair and a raincoat stiff with dirt, the impression might have been of a rubbish-tip ghost, a fragment of walking refuse. Scratching at his tangle of beard, he moved between the mounds, his tattered shoes – the remains of a once-fashionable pair – squelching in the ooze. A sickly sweet smell lingered over the dump as cardboard, wood and twisted metal began their transition into silhouette.

He soon found what he was looking for. It was rusty and all four wheels were missing, its belly resting on the ground. A dead leaf scratched at the flaking roof, then fell into the mud. He allowed his gaze to take in the darkening shape. Peering through the passenger-door window, he looked impassively at the roof lining hanging in shreds, the instrument panel like an empty skull, a few wires straggling as though nerve ends. On the floor lay crystals of windscreen and, as if in mockery, the handbrake was fully applied.

'Would you like a lift?' she asked.

He studied the twisted steering wheel, a small spider busy in the gap. Daylight was fading fast now.

'It's Alan, isn't it? Trouble with your car?'

'I think it's an electrical fault.'

'Jump in. I take it we're going to the same place.'

'Thanks.'

Alan opened the door and climbed in. The engine murmured quietly. The first thing he noticed was her perfume; even as the car accelerated and a breeze washed the air, the fragrance remained. Bright early- morning sunshine slid up the bonnet and onto her dress, its lapels fluttering like wings. They'd met before, briefly, after a lecture, and again at a rather formal party. He knew her name was Stella.

The pungency of the dump re-focussed his mind. Although it was dark now, he could make out a pine table with splayed legs and a washing machine filled with dirt. Moonlight began to sharpen every line and point every angle. The innards of a shattered radio lay spilled nearby. Pieces of the moon were scattered over the flaking bonnet.

'You must have been quick,' said Stella getting into the car. 'Did you get everything?'

'Almost. Then this rain started. We can collect your dress tomorrow.'

'So long as it's ready; I hardly want to get married in jeans.'

Heavy rain battered the windscreen. The windows began to mist up. 'I take it,' she added with a glint in her eye, 'you'll manage to shave for our wedding?'

Alan smiled. 'Maybe. But I'm beginning to enjoy the lazy life, what with your driving me everywhere since we sold my car. Besides, I like watching you change gear; the way you tug down your hem is very modest.

At that moment Stella's foot slipped off the brake. The car lurched forward, a red traffic light refracted in the windscreen's raindrops. Despite the shock, she recovered control and pulled up quickly. She was breathing hard and began to tremble. But, as they'd been at the head of the traffic, no harm was done and she recovered within a few minutes. Alan tried to persuade her to let him drive, but she asserted she was perfectly capable, so he didn't press the point. They continued the journey slowly, Stella blaming her wet shoes. It was only when they stopped outside her home that they discovered the pedal rubber was worn smooth.

That evening, Stella insisted Alan go and buy a new pedal rubber. It was still raining and he didn't feel like going out. They didn't argue, but Stella referred obliquely to Alan's growing laziness and, reluctantly, he put on his coat, found the car keys and stalked out.

It was nearly five miles to the late-night petrol station. Alan thought it possible they might not have the part he wanted. As he began the journey, he wiped condensation from the windscreen and cursed the weather. Cats eyes darted at him from the dark and shattered at the edge of the windscreen. Then he had an idea. Instead of continuing to the petrol station, he pulled onto a track after only a mile.

The rubbish dump was in darkness. He took his torch and umbrella from the back seat and picked his way towards an area designated for scrap cars. Although careful, he couldn't help getting his leather shoes muddy. Soon he found a likely looking wreck and shone his torch through the broken passenger-door window. As he'd hoped, the brake still bore its pedal rubber. The roof- lining hung in shreds. The instrument panel looked like an empty skull, a few wires straggling as though nerve ends.

'Like a lift?' she asked.

'Very funny,' Alan replied as he got in.

'Don't be like that,' pleaded Stella as they drove off. 'Not on our wedding day.'

'Sorry. Nerves, I suppose. I stubbed my toe in the bathroom, couldn't find my tie and almost spilled breakfast in my lap.' He forced himself to relax, then brushed a fleck of dust off his jacket.

Both of them were edgy. But the day was warm, though still damp, and, as they neared the registry office, each began to smile, then joked about breaking with tradition by arriving together. Alan looked at Stella and couldn't help feeling proud; every inch of her was immaculate, not a hair nor a stitch out of place. Her new dress complimented her like a picture in a well-matched frame. She, in her turn, commented on his smart appearance and his new-found adroitness with a razor.

The day rushed past in a whirl of faces and greetings. The small reception at their new flat was full of laughter. Guests, having inspected the presents, were shown all the rooms, each freshly decorated. No finger marks surrounded switches or door knobs, none of the chairs sagged from use and the carpet by each door was unworn. Everything was new: the pine table, the radio, the washing machine, everything.

Alan tried to remember how the argument began. The guests had left and Stella mentioned it was a pity they'd decided to forgo an old-fashioned honeymoon. Alan pointed out how restricted their finances were, that it was better to have the flat. Stella thought she detected resentment that they'd sold his car. Within moments, the tension of the day burst out, their tempers escalating, the flat filled with recriminations. Before either knew what was happening, Stella smashed a plate. Alan swore and swept a pile of presents off the table. At that point, Stella, in tears, snatched up the car keys and ran out of the flat.

It took him a while to realise what had happened. He sat down in one of the new chairs and stared at the debris. The flat seemed unnaturally quiet. He sat there for a long time, daylight from the windows gradually dimming, darkness emptying the room.

His gaze remained fixed. If he saw the now-motionless spider, his expression gave no indication of it. Eventually, his eyes re-focussed of their own accord. Through the web, he could see the brake pedal. Its perished rubber was split in half.

He reached out and fingered the twisted steering wheel, then the hollow instrument panel. Moonlight silvered an area around it, but the hollow was black. Slowly, he withdrew his hand and rubbed his matted beard. The car door creaked open at his push, he stepped into the darkness and began to pick his way back towards the road.

Assault and Bartery

The High Prince of Heuneberg Hill Fort and Ruler of the Upper Danube Celts conveys his salutations to Damonon the Greek, now resident at Tarquinii in Etruria. Greetings.

Noble Damonon, I trust this finds you in good health, rich in the pleasures of life and bathing in sunshine, very little of which we have seen recently in these more northerly latitudes. But more of that in a moment.

My dear Damonon, perhaps you are wondering why this papyrus comes to you – if it arrives at all – in a rain-spotted and blood-soaked condition, carried by a wounded, ragged messenger who is not, in fact, the emissary you sent to me, but one of my own men. Of your emissary, I shall have more to say in a moment.

Worthy Damonon, you know me for a mighty and, I may say, progressive prince. Have I not raised the prestige of Heuneberg so that it can no longer be said the Celts of the Upper Danube are uncivilised? Who installed new smelting furnaces, cut drainage ditches, forbad the limbs of captives to be strewn near drinking water? It was I who imported drills and lathes to re-equip our potters' and weavers' workshops. Through your good office, astute Damonon, I bought black figurines from Greece, Etruscan gold, lignite bracelets and amphorae from Marseilles. And I was well pleased when your emissary described the wonders of Mediterranean architecture and explained how you, enterprising Damonon, could send me, from your newly-built palace, a surveyor who would build my hill fort a defensive wall. It would make me the most powerful man on the Danube. Of your surveyor too, I shall have more to say in a moment.

I hope it has not escaped your attention, affluent Damonon, that history has grown wild in Europe and constantly threatens to burst from the forests, send waves of Celts north and west and even south, perhaps as far as Tarquinii and your own peaceful, lavishly adorned residence so recently acquired as a result of your trading enterprises. This would cause me much grief and I would be inconsolable for minutes on end.

When I inspected my new defensive wall, the pride I felt was inexpressible. Heuneberg was no longer a mere hill fort to be disdained by cultivated southerners. The earlier grumblings of my chiefs had ceased, for the wall was worth every one of the rare wild deer, the carefully bred cattle, the hides and pelts, the snake fibulae, Baltic amber, goblets and plates I paid you. I even dug up the treasure from our nine great burial mounds, including the venerated Hohmichele. With my council and warriors, I processed in full pomp round the wall, the poets singing my praises as I gloried in Mediterranean technology, the impressive, sun-dried mud bricks.

The work was completed not a moment too soon. Even before your emissary and surveyor could depart, a horde of barbarians broke from the surrounding forest. I refer to them as barbarians, despite their being Celts, for, to be candid and all modesty aside, they obviously lacked the cultivation and refinement of the inhabitants of Heuneberg. Their army assembled beneath my new wall. Safely inside, we showered them with missiles and insults, sure of our position.

All of us, that is, except your emissary and your surveyor, discerning Damonon. They alone appeared worried and would not be calmed. Ignoring such weakness, I climbed to the topmost point of the hill fort and awaited the attack. It did not come.

The barbarians, I thought, must be in awe of my formidable wall. They stood motionless, lined up and facing it, but it was not fear I saw on their faces. Experienced and powerful warrior though I am, I confess it was an unnerving experience to behold a whole army with a grin on its face. It was an exceedingly strange sight. We showered and, I may say, rained further insults upon them. All they did was remain quite still, grin and occasionally look up at the sky.

I have never visited Tarquinii, sun-burned Damonon. I am told the sky is always blue and the weather always warm. Here in Heuneberg we are not so fortunate, the climate, as you must know, being more temperate. That is to say, wet.

When, next day, it began to rain, your emissary's legs seemed reluctant to support him and he began to shake uncontrollably. The poor fellow, unused to our weather, must have caught influenza and he retreated into a warm hut. On the second day, when the rain fell much harder, my own legs too had reason to feel weak.

On the third wet day, while the grinning army waded through the porridge of our wall, I had occasion to enquire of your surveyor, not unreasonably I thought, how many defensive, sun-dried mud-brick walls he had successfully constructed north of the Aegean. And, while fleeing across our choked drainage ditches and past our hissing furnaces, admiring as I went, exquisite flagons and muddied fabrics strewn by the sludge-filled potters' and weavers' workshops, I regret to inform you your surveyor might, in heat of the battle, have had his measuring stick thrust down his throat, his arms and legs lopped off and the more personal parts of his anatomy stuck on an ornate, bronze spear.

You will be delighted to learn, wise Damonon, that I and a band of warriors survived the onslaught and managed to wade to the inner keep. To be honest with you, as I know I can, only the unsophisticated would grace this inner defence with the name of keep. It has little that would merit a second glance from a knowledgeable, travelled man like yourself; it boasts no pleasing proportions, stylistic niceties or careful carvings. In truth, its dry stone blocks are not even dressed, nor fitted accurately together. But they are of stone.

It affords me especial pleasure to be able to inform you that your emissary survived and was one of those who took refuge with us in the keep. I cannot adequately express how eagerly we learned of his presence. I shall have more to say of him in a moment. For now, suffice to say my warriors were thankful to be alive and were moved to perform one of our ancient ceremonies. Like you cultivated Greeks, we too have a pantheon of gods, but we tend to retain, rather obstinately, our quaint traditional rites – particularly the fetish of the severed head.

My Hellenic friend, rest assured that most of us in the keep were spared and that the only persons to be slain were all my artisans, all my herdsmen, my farmers, priests, musicians, poets, three-quarters of my spearmen and lesser warriors and all the women and children. Luckily, the civilised elite survived and no-one of any importance was killed. Appreciating my status, the besieging chief, after washing off the mud which covered him head to toe, offered me terms and bade me join him on his intended further advance. This, having considered my severe shortage of weapons, food and prospects, I condescended to do.

I trust, courteous Damonon, having read this missive, you will appreciate my disrupted circumstances and those of this whole region, whose violence has not, as yet, disturbed your own sunny tranquillity. I hope you will readily excuse the slovenliness of my messenger and his blood-soaked appearance. And I hasten to inform you, attentive Damonon, that I am gathering all my strength and resources – those, that is, that are left to me after so much expensive war and trade – to avail myself of the pleasure of a personal visit to you at the very earliest opportunity.

Also, Greek, I have despatched to you, via several different routes, your emissary who, regrettably, did not survive our very thorough surgery intended to cure him permanently of his influenza.

> From the ex-High Prince of Heuneberg Hill Fort, and now member of the expanding Upper Danube Celts, to Damonon the Greek. Salutations.

Postscript

Although it happened many years ago, it haunts my mind. I delivered a letter to a derelict house.

I was new to both the job and the valley and, although the Christmas rush was only just starting, finding some of the addresses had put me behind. I should have simply returned the letter to the sorting office but, with a twinge of guilt, I told myself I was late. I pushed it through the letterbox and heard it fall inside. Hurrying on with my round, I forgot the incident – until five days later I pulled out of my bag another letter for the same address.

Standing in front of the stone house, I pondered for a moment. The place stood by itself and once, long ago when the mine was worked, it must have been considered a cut above the terraced cottages further down the valley. Now, through broken windows, I could glimpse peeling walls and chinks of light where slates were missing.

I was tempted to send the second letter after the first, but my conscience got the better of me. I decided to collect the first letter and return them both to the office. The bushes which had overgrown the front path rattled as I pushed my way to the front door. It was locked, but I had no difficulty reaching through its broken stained glass and locating the latch. I pushed open the door and stepped into a narrow hallway. Scattered at my feet were old circulars and a few official brown envelopes delivered before my time. But the letter I had delivered wasn't there.

It was the smell of the place that seemed wrong. I had a slight cold and thought I must be imagining it; instead of damp and mustiness, the place smelled of wood polish, tile stain and flowers.

I checked whether the letter had fallen between the floorboards, but the gaps were clogged with dirt. Straightening up, I concluded I'd wasted enough time and told myself at least I'd made the effort. But a strange, uneasy feeling held me there. I looked at the letter I'd brought with me; it was addressed to a Miss D. Owen. Its careful, old-fashioned writing stared back at me. And then I did an odd thing. I let the letter fall from my hand. It hit the floor and lay on the circulars. I pulled the door shut behind me and left.

Walking down to Capel Hendre, my mind still inhabited the derelict house. I couldn't help wondering about Miss D. Owen. Mechanically, I delivered the day's post to a row of terraced houses. At first, I convinced myself I'd left the letter because I hadn't returned the first one. Then I admitted to myself I'd succumbed to sheer laziness. But I wasn't convinced that was all there was to it.

My thoughts were interrupted while I delivered a letter to twenty-two Bryn Street. As I reached forward to push the letter into the letterbox, the door opened. I found myself face to face with a severe-looking man of about sixty-five. I smiled automatically and made some remark about good timing but, instead of replying, he snatched the letter from my hand and disappeared back inside the house. His brusqueness surprised me. I'd found everyone in the area friendly. From the envelope, I knew his name was Donald Merion. He hadn't spoken a word, nor had a flicker of a smile crossed his face. Also, he'd been wearing a coat and had clearly been about to go out.

I shrugged off the encounter as unimportant. During the afternoon, after I'd finished work, I set out on foot to meet some new friends I'd made. My route took me past the derelict house. When I drew level with it, I stopped. Even now, I can't be sure why. It wasn't that I'd definitely changed my mind about the letter. The place nagged at me. Whatever the reason, I pushed past the bushes again and opened the door. The same fresh smell greeted me as I stooped to pick up the letter. The letter wasn't there.

Each day that passed made my job easier. I grew familiar with the streets and the eccentric numbering of some of the houses. I enjoyed the freshness of the sharpening air and the hues of the surrounding hills. But every time I passed the derelict house, my eyes were drawn towards it. I had the feeling of being watched, as though someone resided behind those cracked windows. There were various reasons to account for the disappearance of the letters, of course – kids, a sheltering tramp, a prospective buyer – but somehow I wasn't convinced.

It was exactly a week later that the third letter arrived. It was this letter that drew me beyond the point of mere speculation. As before, it was addressed to Miss D. Owen and in the same careful handwriting. I felt distinctly uneasy as I approached the path. Pale sunshine glinted on slivers of glass, highlighted rotting window frames, collected in loose gutters. I opened the door and walked in.

I toyed with the letter in my hands as I inspected each room. The downstairs front room contained a few pieces of splintered furniture. The back room was empty, apart from a roll of mouldering carpet propped up in one corner. Rising damp blackened the walls beneath the windows. In the kitchen, the sink had been smashed.

I climbed the stairs. Outdated wiring clung awkwardly to the walls, smashed light fittings hanging uselessly. Cracks zigzagged the plaster and, in every corner, ancient cobwebs sagged with dirt. There was no sign of recent habitation.

I don't remember actually making the decision but, standing in one of the forlorn bedrooms, I knew what I was going to do. I slid an index finger under the flap of the envelope and eased the surfaces apart. The flap came free without damaging the paper.

Inside were two sheets of notepaper, folded once. The neat handwriting matched the envelope, but it was the writer's address that came as a shock; it was twenty-two Bryn Street. I turned quickly to the second sheet; the letter signed off with 'Your ever-loving Donald.'

Suppressing the urge to leave, I read the letter. 'My dearest Delia,' it began. I felt a nervousness deep in my stomach as I continued to the end of the second page. It was a love letter. That the writer was deeply in love with Delia was obvious from every line. He expressed his joy at their recent outing, but most of all at her acceptance of his proposal of marriage. The ceremony would take place on his twenty-second birthday.

My gaze fell on the garden outside the window as I thought of Donald Merion. I saw again those possessed eyes. The letter referred to the apple tree in the garden, the place where Donald had proposed to her. The apple tree still stood there, but it was leafless and no decaying apples were littered round its base. And then, stupidly, I realised I'd overlooked the most important thing; the letter had a date on the first page. The eleventh of November, nineteen forty-three.

I stared uncomprehendingly at the garden, its brambles arching over unkempt grass, a fence leaning like a comb in unruly hair. A sharp noise brought me back to reality.

I froze. The front door had banged closed. Suddenly I couldn't understand why I was there, why I was in a dilapidated bedroom with someone else's letter in my hands. Downstairs, all was quiet. I couldn't hear any footsteps.

An aroma of flowers seemed to drift up the staircase. Mingled with it came the scent of wax. I waited. I replaced the letter in its envelope and re-sealed it. Two paces took me to the bedroom door. I peered round the door jamb. The circulars still lay near the bottom of the stairs. The front door was closed.

I took a deep breath, then bounded noisily down the stairs. 'Hello,' I called cheerily, 'anyone about?'

The silence swallowed my false heartiness. The front room was empty. So were the back room and kitchen. The back door was still bolted. Although window panes were broken, no space was large enough for someone to climb through.

I stood still and listened again. Had the sunlight made a noise as it fell, I'd have heard it. A spider couldn't have moved without my sensing it. Somewhere outside, in another world, a bird sang. It crossed my mind that someone might have opened the front door to check for letters. And then, as though it was the most natural thing in the world, I reached into my bag for a bundle of post. It was the bundle for Bryn Street. A line that I'd read in the letter came back to me; 'This is our only means of contact now.'

In the bundle, I found a letter for Donald Merion, just as I'd known I would. The address was printed in block capitals and the stamp showed yesterday's date. All conscience gone, I eased open the flap and withdrew the contents. I unfolded the letter and Delia Owen stared up at me.

Despite the blurred greyness of the photograph, Delia smiled easily through the years. Her hair bunched behind her head, hands resting casually in the lap of her W.R.A.F. uniform, she looked both smart and attractive. Her collar and tie appeared uncomfortable, but the ill-fitting skirt and jacket didn't conceal her figure. The photograph was creased and well-thumbed. She'd signed it on the back, 'Your own Delia'.

The envelope had been posted locally. I read her letter slowly. The pages had obviously been written long ago, the blue ink turning coppery. She told Donald of her love, of how she longed for their reunion. Her posting to London had been unexpected, but their planned marriage needn't be delayed for long. She couldn't divulge too much about her activities, just that she was pushing toy aircraft about on a map of Southern England. There were other details, followed by a brief description of the excitement and fear she felt during bombing raids.

When I left the house, I felt ashamed, a voyeur who had witnessed something he'd no right to see. Treading on the circulars, I closed the door of the derelict house for the last time. I looked back and imagined the place as it had been forty or fifty years before. I could imagine the hedges trimmed and the lawn cut, nettles and weeds cleared away. In my mind, I repainted the woodwork, repaired the roof and windows. The apple tree sagged with fruit. Flowers grew and supplied the house with colour and the waxed wooden furniture shone. I thought of the face that had smiled from one of the windows and then I thought of the features of the occupant of twenty-two Bryn Street.

I continued on my round and delivered Donald Merion's letter. And every week afterwards I delivered a letter for Delia at the derelict house, each envelope addressed in the same careful hand.

Although the reply to twenty-two Bryn Street always arrived in a fresh envelope, I knew the contents never changed. I left the same letter at the same house for a further six years, at which time Donald Merion died and the letters stopped.

Finisher

Remote Farm
Herefordshire

Celtic Racing Ltd
Cardiff

Dear Mr. Hughs,

I quit. Yesterday was the final straw. I resign. As of now, you can find a new first-string driver for your Formula One team – and we all know who *that* will be, don't we?

Duggan, my so-called team mate, has beaten me only once this year; I finished ahead of him in the Belgian Grand Prix, the Italian Grand Prix and the Australian Grand Prix and I've moved steadily up the championship table. So I was especially keyed-up for yesterday; what a perk for the season if I could win the Welsh Grand Prix.

Of course, I'd suspected a conspiracy for some time. What I didn't suspect was the depth to which you and Duggan would sink. However, I focused on the race. Centred on Brynamman, the Welsh Grand Prix is a very demanding circuit. As I put on my helmet and took my place on the grid, I concentrated on the coming challenge. Even so, I happened to notice Duggan watching me more intently than usual.

I didn't actually become aware something was crawling up my left leg until the first bend. Not being well-read in natural science, I couldn't tell whether it was an asp, an adder or an anaconda. Nor was I fortunate enough to have a 'Collins Wildlife Pocketbook' about my person – despite being in the ideal place to purchase one, having just crashed through the Post Office window at seventy miles an hour – so I couldn't look up the snake's precise markings, very fine though I'm sure they were.

That I and my car escaped virtually unscathed is a miracle – although the Postmaster might hold a different view, my exit being via his living-room window, greenhouse and rose garden. I don't know what happened to the snake; it's probably racing for safety to the nearest jungle.

By sheer skill and determination, I clawed my way back to the leaders. Ahead, I could make out some of the opposition, including that gum-chewing, gear-missing cockpit-spit, Duggan. I turned off my DRS and conserved fuel. On the straight from Glanamman, I employed my razor-sharp brain to calculate I had enough fuel to pit on the pre-arranged lap. So, it was with some annoyance, as you can imagine, that I found the throttle stuck wide open.

The left-hander at Gwaun Cau Gurwen is almost a hairpin. At a pinch, it can be taken at forty miles an hour. Approaching it, therefore, at one hundred and eighty, I don't mind admitting I nearly scorched my fireproof underwear.

It was only my quick thinking and the flimsy gates of Gwaun Cau Gurwen level crossing that saved Dinefwr Council's new and, in this case, appropriately-sited, public conveniences from certain destruction.

Speeding along the railway line, my wheels locked on the rails, I took the opportunity to clamber out of the cockpit and onto the bonnet. I located the throttle mechanism, reached underneath and removed what might have been tar or rubber. Or chewing gum.

Unfortunately, I wasn't quite back inside the cockpit when the coal wagons appeared. They were loaded with bags of coal from Tairgwaith. Tairgwaith, as you probably know, is an opencast mine. I had never seen its workings and machinery. On landing, I was able to take a close look at these interesting operations, although, travelling at a hundred miles an hour and steering with my left foot, the inspection was necessarily brief.

Amazingly, the car was still functioning and I determined not to let minor setbacks defeat me. I jolted my way back to the road – albeit via the scenic, snow-covered summit of Garreg-Lwyd – and, relying on experience to evaluate such finely-judged factors as tyre wear – and noticing I hadn't got any – I decided a pit-stop seemed advisable.

I arrived at Brynamman. My car roared into the pits. The main question, as I delivered extraneous bags of coal, was could the highly-trained mechanics save me precious time? Could they change the wheels faster than their record of four point two seconds?

While waiting for them to finish their cigarettes and their chat about summer holidays, it crossed my mind I wasn't receiving first-string-driver attention. I ventured to mention this. In fact, if I hadn't called the A.A., I'd still be there now.

Rejoining the course, there was nothing for it but to go flat out. I gradually made up for lost time. The car's titanium undershield struck showers of sparks from the road, despite Dinefwr Council's renowned billiard-table-smooth workmanship.

I began to catch up. I screeched past the poorer-aspirated cars. I overtook the Brazilian World Champion. At last, only Duggan was in front of me. He could see me in his mirrors. Only ten laps to go. I drew closer. Taking every inch of the racing line, we sped on. He was clearly pushing hard; his exhaust got blacker.

A lot blacker. Despite the sunshine, everything went dark. It was like driving at night – or through oily, black smoke. As Duggan pulled away, I'm almost sure he gave a cheery wave. But I continued to race flat out, so knew he couldn't be far ahead. I concentrated on the white lines. To my relief, a couple of marshals appeared out of the gloom and directed me. They seemed vaguely familiar – perhaps it was the casual way they held their cigarettes – but I didn't have time to think about it. Foot hard down, I powered on. I was determined not to let Duggan win. The smoke started to clear. It was when I overtook a battered mini that I suspected foul play. Any remaining doubts disappeared when I read a sign welcoming me to Herefordshire.

Running out of fuel was the final straw. Thumbing a lift, I got lucky, despite the humiliation of being towed by a mini. Actually, its owner is a genial and refreshingly genuine chap. He's a farmer. Not only has he put me up, but he's also given me work.

If you want the remains of your Formula One car, you'd better arrange to collect them. I suggest you don't send the new Welsh Champion. It would be so tragic if Duggan, the new star, was accidentally run over by a tractor half a dozen times. Despite its leisurely pace, I haven't quite got the hang of the controls.

You can keep your high-speed, split-second world. You can keep the stench of exhaust, racing oil and scorched tyres. In just a matter of hours, I've been reminded of other smells; cut grass, woodland after rain and even manure.

Which reminds me; Duggan will no doubt be racing for you for some years. Give him this message from me; it's my revenge. When he's finished racing, when he's had his nerves and eardrums battered beyond repair, tell him he won't be able to hear a thrush or lark or wood pigeon, as I do now. Tell him the countryside isn't at its best at two hundred miles an hour, that spring and autumn pass quickly enough without any help, that a tractor is plenty fast enough.

Tell him I won.

Yours sincerely,

N.M.

Joint Account

I, Craig Wheeler, wish to make a statement. I have been told I do not have to do so, but that anything I write may be used in evidence. I'll set down all I remember, although I'm still suffering from the effects of concussion. My memory's improving, but I still hear voices. It's an odd sensation. It's like driving a car without being fully in control. I'll set down what happened, just as it comes. I won't try to dress it up.

(Convincing, isn't he?)

I'm not sure where to begin. I can hardly believe it's me lying here, propped up in a counterpaned bed. My head's aching and the pastel walls seem strangely vivid. The day before yesterday; a matter of forty hours. It's as if it happened to someone else.

(Just as it comes? Won't dress it up? Take my advice; don't believe a word of it. He's just softening you up.)

My difficulty's not only to assemble the facts, but to face them.

(First, no doubt, he'll set the scene and win your confidence with his openness.)

It happened in a house in Bryn Street. As you might know, Bryn Street's just dingy rows of terraces on the outskirts of Swansea. I was renting a small flat on the ground floor. It was dismal. The whole place needed repairs and my windows looked onto a rubbish-strewn railway line. The roof leaked, the walls didn't so much need re-pointing as rebuilding and the garden was a collection of rusting prams and Coke tins. I suppose I shouldn't complain; there were other people worse off than me.

(Touching, isn't it? Got your hanky ready? Personally, I find him a bit obvious, but then I know him better than you do.)

Carys, for instance. She rented the flat directly above mine. I immediately took to Carys.

(That's me.)

I still seem to sense her presence. She was mid-twenties – a couple of years younger than me – and, when she wasn't in one of her depressions, she had the most buoyant personality you could wish to meet.

(Who, me? That's not what he said when he was drunk – which is a hell of a lot more often than he'll admit.)

I'd better admit straight away I drank quite a lot.

(O.K., so I was wrong. Watch him though; he's clever at disarming people. If he says he's going to be honest –)

To be honest –

(– it means he's going to lie.)

To be honest, I felt a bit isolated. I first met Carys on the stairs and straight away sensed a kindred spirit. Although she had large, sad eyes, she usually laughed a lot and could be stimulating company.

(Where's the lie? All this is true. Still, if he's going to praise me, who am I to interrupt?)

I think it was her sense of the ludicrous that appealed most. When we knew each other better, we'd curl up at the silliest jokes. She'd roll about, tears in her eyes and helpless with laughter. But occasionally she suffered from deep depressions – they were so black they used to frighten me. They weren't frequent, I'm glad to say, but – there's no point in hiding it from you – Carys was an alcoholic.

(What! Rubbish! All right, I drank a bit but –)

She could drink me under the table. She told me she'd been on residential cures, but none of them had worked for long. The fact is, I'm afraid she regularly stole drink from supermarkets.

(That's not true! He's accusing me of his own crimes!)

You know what it's like the morning after? Carys didn't. While you were blearily reaching for your alarm clock, Carys was reaching for another bottle. Day after day. When she was on a binge, there was no telling how long it would last. You'd have thought she'd drink herself unconscious and that would be that. Not Carys. The human body's very resilient – hers was anyway. A doze for a couple of hours, then she'd start again.

(And if you believe that, you'll believe anything. You know why he sounds so convincing, don't you? He believes his own fabrications. He's frightened to face the truth.)

I don't deny I drank a lot too, but I did it in moderation.

(How can you drink a lot in moderation? He downed it like a plug hole. There were times when he couldn't go two minutes without reaching for a glass. What's more, drink sometimes made him violent. Well, I warned you; Craig's a liar.)

Worse – and I don't like having to denigrate her – Carys was a congenital liar.

(Of all the barefaced nerve!)

She'd be telling you about her day, and suddenly you'd realise she was in a world of her own. Pure invention. It wasn't easy to spot at first because her normal day was often wild anyway. She didn't have a job – she couldn't hold one down – but that doesn't mean she was broke; I'll tell you why in a minute. Sometimes, after work, I'd fetch her from the betting office – a scruffy, smoky place littered with screwed up paper – and she'd talk about odds and form all the way home.

(In case you missed the hint, he's let you know how distasteful he finds gambling. Cunning.)

I was working in a supermarket in Castle Street.

(Oh yeah? So who had the opportunity to steal booze? If I let him waffle on long enough, he's bound to trip himself up. Liars always do.)

I wasn't exactly a model employee. I was forever arriving late and making excuses for having days off. And the excuses I made up, well, I blush to recall them. But I didn't dare lose the job, otherwise I'd have to live on my newly-acquired savings: four thousand pounds from selling my dilapidated, but much-loved, Lotus Seven sports car. I kept looking at my bank book, just for the pleasure of reading the figures. Carys had done even better: a couple of months after we met, she'd been left ten thousand pounds by an aunt – an abstemious one actually – and she drew out the lot simply to revel in it. To us, these sums were fortunes. But drink, even if you steal it, becomes an expensive hobby. Add Carys's gambling and it was clear her money wouldn't last long.

(Sorry – I was dropping off. Craig does go on a bit sometimes. Just like some of our evenings together. No doubt he'll get to the point soon.)

Carys is dead now.

(That was a bit abrupt!)

It's so difficult to accept. In a way, she still seems close. Oh Carys, why did it have to happen?

(You tell *me*.)

I need to understand it, get it clear in my mind. I need to make sense of it.

(Me too. Nail-biting, isn't it? The tension's not too much for you? Hanging on to his desperate need to communicate, to unburden himself? Me neither. We know better than to be fooled so easily.)

We used to spend hours discussing our circumstances. What should we do for the best? One suggestion was we move in together to cut expenses. Another was to pool our money in a joint account; the idea was that, if two signatures were required for withdrawals, each of us could restrain the other. I rejected that idea.

(*Who* rejected that idea?)

We even joked about blowing the lot on a trip to Turkey. It was a country that had magic appeal for both of us. But, as I told Carys only two nights ago, the solution to her problems didn't lie in dreaming. We were sprawled on the carpet in my flat.

(At last.)

When I say carpet, I mean a faded pattern of stains puddled with threadbare patches.

(Oh, oh. Sounds like a bout of metaphors on the way.)

The curtains were drawn. They billowed with each gust from the ill-fitting windows. Their flowers sucked up moisture like the real things, except the moisture was from the damp walls.

(He used to go on like that for ages, if I let him. No wonder I suffered from depressions. I notice he hasn't mentioned his poems. At first, he recited them to me, but later he kept them to himself. I don't know why. Perhaps my fits of uncontrolled laughter had something to do with it.)

We must have looked a funny sight. There we were, huddled in front of my electric fire, its glowing bar drawing us like a magnet, with Carys's money scattered over the floor. We rolled in it and threw it into the air. Carys had been drinking for two days. I don't deny that I too, in fact –

(A dead giveaway – like 'to be honest'.)

- had been drinking as well. To be honest, more than was good for me. Sleet rattled on the window. Carys took out a couple of her poems and read them to me. They were awful. I don't know much about poetry, but I know hers was embarrassingly bad.

(Thanks, Craig.)

We'd eaten a meal earlier – some days Carys didn't bother – which I'd brought home from the supermarket. I usually cooked our meals.

(Ha!)

My head's aching again. It's not that I'm holding back; I need to get things in order. The shock of what happened forces me to keep questioning myself.

(Here we go; soul-searching time. I should go and make a cup of tea if I were you.)

I was tired. I wasn't thinking as clearly as usual.

(Here come the excuses.)

It's not that I'm trying to excuse anything. I won't alter a word of what took place.

(As I say, here come the excuses.)

I tried to discuss investment with her. It was impossible. She persuaded me to join her in a sort of snowball fight with the banknotes. We romped like children. Although Carys appeared flippant – you may laugh at my amateur psychiatry –

(I am.)

– I'm sure her flippancy concealed something dark inside her she was frightened of.

(He sounds so reasonable, doesn't he? Paradoxically, drunks can be experts at sounding reasonable.)

To tell you the truth – I don't want you to think I'm bending the facts to show myself in the best light – I didn't love Carys. I needed her sometimes, and she needed me, but I didn't love her.

(I loved him. I really loved him. Would I admit that if I intended to fool you? Of course not. Far easier to joke about it and laugh it off. Listen to me, then decide who's telling the truth. Reverse what he's told you. It was *I* who worked in the supermarket in Castle Street and Craig who had the serious drink problem. He told me he'd been on residential cures, but none of them had worked for long. All this about selling a sports car is pure invention; he didn't own a car. As for a Lotus, well, is it likely? It's true I liked to gamble a little, but he makes it sound as though I spent half my life in the betting shop. Most of my betting was on card games – like the one we played that night.)

I never really knew where I was with her. So much of her was a facade, so how could I be sure her deeper feelings weren't false too? If you ask me, her depressions were a kind of self-inflicted punishment. I'll tell you something else – something I never expected to have to divulge –

(Craig, no! You promised!)

I'm sure she was telling me the truth because she showed me the scar. She'd attempted it about a year before I moved into Bryn Street. A razor blade. Just one wrist. Apparently, she hadn't cut deeply enough.
(The one time I want him to lie, he tells the truth.)

Can you imagine how I felt when she had one of her depressions? She'd disappear into her room upstairs and lock the door. There was no telling whether it would last hours or days. I tried to talk to her through the door; the best I could hope for was a brief response which at least told me she was coping. And then, quite suddenly, she'd reappear, freshly showered, her face animated again. The funny thing was, she never touched alcohol during these depressions; she'd return with a joke about gasping for a drink.

(Now he's back to his psychopathic lying. Meanwhile, the stakes in our card game were getting higher.)

We were playing three- card Brag. Suddenly she said, 'You wanted to talk investment. O.K., we'll talk investment. I've got a plan.' Those were her exact words. 'I've got a plan.' I don't want to mislead you by recalling it inaccurately.

(God forbid.)

If only I'd known what she had in mind.

(Me too.)

'This isn't one of your jokes, is it?' I asked. 'You've really thought of a sound investment?' 'Oh, it's sound all right,' she replied. 'Very sound. For one of us.' Despite being a bit muddled with drink, I got the meaning straight away. For *one* of us. It was startling. The trouble is, it wasn't as startling as it ought to have been. I'm aware it would be sensible to exaggerate now; I should describe how I ranted and protested – and I *did*.

(Of *course* you did.)

But, somehow, not as much as I should have done. I refused, I promise you. But, well, she taunted and mocked and, what with the drink...

(Don't tell us you gave in?)

Pride, I suppose. She went on about how each of us was merely buying time; we were both failures.

(Speak for yourself.)

How the cliché about money not buying happiness was a fallacy. How, with extra money, the average person's opportunities multiplied – even for finding love. She challenged me; she picked up my bank book and threw it into my lap. Then she scooped up armfuls of notes and swamped the kitty with them. Looking for a way out, I argued it was unfair to bet my four thousand pounds against her ten. She dismissed that by saying she'd have four cards to my three. I decided to call her bluff. In a blur of bravado and alcohol, I tossed my bank book into the kitty.

(He didn't *have* four thousand pounds. He reassembles events to suit himself; it's an inner compulsion. When I visited him at the supermarket, he'd invent little stories about his workmates – no wait. What I mean is, when he visited *me* at the supermarket. Damn.)

I refilled our glasses while Carys thoroughly shuffled the cards.

(Look, you mustn't read too much into my slip. It was only an inversion of the words. It could happen to anyone. I'm not denying we made a bet; in fact, to be honest, I readily agreed to it. I staked all my money and Craig asked what he could possibly bet to match it. So I told him; if I won, he'd have to stop drinking, get a job and hold it down.)

I couldn't believe she'd go through with it. I expected her to roll over laughing and back down.

('The winnings could pay for a cure,' he said; 'a cure that really works.')

The winnings could pay for a cure, I said; a cure that really works.

(We're agreed on something then.)

Despite the wine, I reasoned it out in my mind. I made her agree that, if she won, she'd spend most of the money on a cure. If she lost, I'd simply say I'd been joking. It was easy. Besides, with four cards to my three, she stood a good chance. Supplies were running low – by now it was early morning – so we agreed to an extra condition; the winner was to brave the weather and go for more drink. An Asian shop near Swansea station stayed open all night. We decided it on a single hand. Carys dealt.

(We picked up our cards and huddled them close.)

Carys selected three cards from her four. I looked at my hand, then at her face.

(I looked at my hand, then at his face. He smiled.)

She smiled. She'll call it off now, I thought. But she didn't.

(He'll call it off now, I thought. But he didn't. Laughing, I rolled over.)

One by one, I put down my cards: a ten, a seven. And then another ten. She stared at them. 'A pair of tens,' she said quietly. 'Not a bad hand.' Then she looked straight into my eyes and said, 'While you're at the shop, you can buy me some cigarettes.' I immediately called the bet off. I told her it had been a joke.

(The moment I'd glanced at my cards, I knew I'd won. That's why I rolled over laughing. But he said the whole thing had been a joke. I said a bet's a bet.)

She got annoyed and insisted I'd won. She scooped the pile of notes towards me, knocked back a glassful of wine and said she'd no intention of taking a cure. I snatched up her cards; all she had was a king high. I refused to take the money and swore all I cared about was her. Look, despite what I wrote before, I loved her. I really loved her. Would I admit that if I intended to fool you, if I were lying?

(My hero. Don't overdo it, Craig; you'll make your readers queasy.) The truth is, I'd tried to keep my distance. I could see the whole set-up was trouble. But relationships seldom work out as planned and I found I cared too much. Some things can't be faked.

I put on my coat and walked to the all-night shop. On the way, I reasoned it wouldn't be difficult to return her money; I'd persuade her to have another bet. I'd find a way. But, when I got back, the world had changed. It was an unfamiliar place.

Sometimes, when you lose someone, they still seem close, as though lingering. Suddenly, all I feel is emptiness. I can't sense her presence.

She'd actually done it. There are no words. I stood in the doorway, unable to move. The carpet really was puddled. I couldn't take it in – not all at once. For some reason, I remember trivial things, like the music from the radio and dropping the plastic bag – I actually worried about crushing her cigarettes. When I could move, I edged towards her. It didn't need a doctor to tell me it was too late. Just one wrist. The kitchen knife. I'm not sure what I did. I think I spoke to her. Then I noticed a card. Of all things, I noticed a playing card jutting from her pocket. It was a king. And then I understood. At that moment it was clear. She'd cheated. She'd had a plan, just as she said; she'd lost deliberately. Deny it, Carys; say it isn't true.

(It isn't true.)

After that, the bits that come back are vague. I placed Carys on the bed, as though she'd be more comfortable there. She didn't wake up. Stupidly, I thought if she did, she'd only open another bottle and I didn't want that. I remember gathering up the notes. In a way, I suppose I was tidying up. Some of the notes were red. It crossed my mind they were the wrong colour, but I was too dazed to puzzle over it.

The next thing I remember is waking up here in hospital. A policeman questioned me. He said I'd been involved in a car crash, that I'd been driving a Lotus Seven. Enquiries had revealed I'd paid cash for it that morning. He told me about Carys. I couldn't think straight. The policeman knew more about me than *I* did; he'd checked with my landlord and my employers at the supermarket.

(Oh well, I suppose that clarifies *that* point.)

The policeman knew all about Carys's alcoholism and medical history; also about her convictions for stealing, of course. It was painful to hear these things confirmed.

(It looks as though Craig was right; I must be a congenital liar. Perhaps I altered things because I found them unacceptable. Lying's like laughing; both make the world seem better than it is.)

The police say I must have driven from Swansea to Bristol and then followed the A36 towards Southampton. Maybe I was heading for the ferry terminal; I can't remember. It's difficult to imagine where I thought I was making for.

(Turkey perhaps?)

When the policeman returned, his attitude was more formal. He said there were certain queries about Carys's death and my actions.

I was told a policeman would be stationed in the corridor. I'm a suspect, yet I've no recollection of buying the Lotus or being involved in a crash. I'm sure I wasn't trying to flee the country. Any inconsistency in my actions must be due to concussion.

(Want a bet? No, perhaps not; the last one wasn't too successful, was it?)

I've written down all I can recall at the moment. Believe me, I've told you the truth.

(Some of it, yes. And I've lied. But the part I haven't told – the true part – will be told by the evidence. How could you do it, Craig? Forensic have found the bruises; and they can tell the difference between a wrist that's cut when someone's alive or when already dead. I can understand the violence, but not this. To do it afterwards, coldly… How could you, Craig? How could you?)

I must stop now and try to rest. I want to sleep, but Carys won't let me. It's more than a headache now; she won't leave my mind. She'll never leave my mind.

Nightfall

I, Glen Deacon, wish to make a statement. I have been told I need not make one unless I wish to do so, but that what I say may be used in evidence.

> He offered to write it down for me. I said no; that if an English teacher can't write his own statement, he shouldn't be teaching. Maybe I imagined the look of contempt that crossed his face. Angry at my gaucheness, I took out a pen. Nothing happened. For a while I gazed at the blank pages and sat there like an examinee who doesn't understand the question.

On the night of July 3rd. at about eight o'clock, I left Brandon Hall, where I am employed as a teacher. I had finished my duties and did not feel like staying in my room.

> Use simple language. Always answer the question. Show you know the subject. But I don't. All I feel is confusion. But they're not much interested in feelings; all they want is their precious narrative.

I walked to The Three Bells, a public house just outside school bounds. I had decided to see whether any members of staff were there; at weekends, a few of us used it as a second common-room. Janette, our matron, occasionally spent an evening there.

> Occasionally? She almost lived there. At twenty-five she was young to be such a heavy drinker. But I suppose I didn't do too badly myself, and I was only a couple of years older. Janette and I got on well. She got on well with most people; they liked her pertness and laughter. Still, the police don't want to know what we are; only what we do.

The Three Bells was busy. Some of the staff from school were there, including Janette, and I joined them. We became quite boisterous as the night went on. I drank more than usual. The time passed quickly and, although it was late, the landlord, who knew our group well, let us continue drinking. I found myself talking to Janette.

How you 'find yourself' talking to someone, I'm not sure. Anyway, in this case, it was deliberate. I quite fancied Janette; not inordinately, but I liked her vivacity – not to mention her slim figure. We played a sort of game; it involved swopping gossip about who was reported to be sleeping with whom, which members of staff were creeping the night-time corridors, and in which direction. Part of the game was that we reserved information about our own activities; in my case it wasn't difficult because there weren't any. But Janette liked to tease me about Andrea. I suppose I can't put off mentioning Andrea any longer.

It was late when I left. I think it was about one o'clock. Janette and a few others remained and seemed set to continue drinking. I was definitely affected by the alcohol I had consumed. I walked back unsteadily to Brandon Hall and went up to my room. I got into bed and fell asleep immediately.

Andrea was one of my forth-formers. She was fourteen, intelligent, a hard worker and, as Janette loved to remind me, had a crush on me. I can't deny I was flattered, nor that it was obvious to everyone she was my favourite. I admit we even flirted a little, in a harmless way. But that's all it was. Andrea had a passion for English Literature which matched my own. On the evening of July 3rd. she brought the prep' books to my room – she was class monitor – and she began talking about Donne's erotic poetry. While she made my pot of tea, we moved on to some of Byron's celebrations of sexuality. For a fourteen-year-old, she could discuss these topics with considerable maturity, but she wasn't afraid to laugh either; she enjoyed the subject-matter and saw no reason to hide the fact. Although I ignored them, Andrea slipped in a few intimate remarks – she probably thought she was being subtle – one of which included drawing close and asking for an opinion on her new perfume. It smelled a little sickly but, disingenuously, I told her I liked it. She said it was called 'Nightfall'.

Something – a noise, I think – woke me. I was very groggy from the drink. The room was in darkness, but I could make out a pale, slender shape. It approached me and, before I realised what was happening, slipped into bed beside me.

I resisted – I'm sure I did. I spoke, but her lips stopped me. I pulled back, but her arms hung on; then her naked body pressed close. I hesitated, dizzy. Within moments, her hands were exploring. My own responded. I touched. She responded with more encouragement and, suddenly, it was too late to stop. Light-headedly, I sensed I should pull away; I recognise, now, that it only enhanced it. Soon I was kissing, cupping, gripping, all the while her body moving uninhibitedly. She sensed a moment of pain as I entered her, but pulled me on, and we lost ourselves in each other, the excitement, the sublime giving and taking.

We had sexual intercourse.

I woke slowly the next morning. I felt warm and relaxed. Then, suddenly, the night flooded back. I sat up sharply. I was alone. Early morning sunshine laid my shadow on the pillow. For a while I remained still. My eyes were stinging but, in my fear, I ignored them. Afraid of certainty, yet pulled down as if by a compelling force, my face gradually grew closer to the pillow. A sweet scent greeted me; it was called 'Nightfall'.

Next morning I went down to breakfast. I do not remember who was there, except that half way through, Mr. Jones, the mathematics master, hurried in and spoke in urgent whispers to Mr. Meakin, the assistant headmaster. The time would have been about half past eight. Mr. Meakin left with Mr. Jones.

I was in the staff common-room when I heard. The news almost paralysed me. Shock waves were already spreading through the school; Andrea was in hospital. No-one seemed clear about what had happened; all that was certain was she'd been found at the bottom of some stairs. A cleaner had stumbled on her early that morning. We asked how she was, but the assistant headmaster said he'd tell us as soon as he had news. Concussion was mentioned. So were various theories about how it had happened. That she'd fallen was obvious, though why she'd been wandering the night-time corridors wasn't; rumours and gossip spread. A police car was parked outside the Hall. I was in a state of panic.

During the morning, I was interviewed by a police officer. I found it difficult to concentrate on his questions.

Textbook in hand, I stood in front of the fourth form. I must have appeared disoriented. I kept staring at Andrea's empty desk and I imagined her gazing steadily back. Was she smiling? Her features danced before me. Her bare arms rested on the desk. Her crisp blouse suggested – but I baulked, alarmed, ashamed. The direction my thoughts turned, even now, sickened me. I wanted to dismiss the events of the night, deny them completely.

The officer explained they were trying to establish what had happened the previous night. They wanted to find out why Andrea had been found so far from her dormitory; why she had been found at the bottom of the stairs that led to the third floor. He asked me which floor my room was on. I told him it was on the third.

Child abuser. The idea horrified me. Misuse of authority. Surely the officer had noticed my guilt, my self-loathing? Fourteen years old. I remembered the 'monsters' of the popular press. I wondered how I, who'd never contemplated harming a child, could possibly have done it. But that only triggered a frantic searching; in my panic, I began to question what I'd thought of as caring; I sought hidden wishes and desires. What made it all so much worse – what I wanted to forget – was that it had been good. It shouldn't have been; it should have been vile. I kept picturing her sitting impassively at her desk.

He asked whether my relationship with Andrea was close.

I seemed to hear her laughing.

I replied that we got on well and that she was a model pupil. I asked whether I could visit her in hospital.

What does a teacher say to a pupil he's seduced? But no, I hadn't seduced her. The fact was – the fact was, I was desperate for an excuse. I blamed alcohol; I blamed inexperience. What had begun as a harmless flirtation had escalated into – had escalated.

The officer said that would be all. As I was leaving, he added that he would want to see me again.

Instead of returning to the common-room, I wandered through the school grounds. I had a free period before lunch, but it would have made no difference if I hadn't. I wondered what Andrea would say when she regained consciousness. Wandering into the woods, I wished I could lose myself. It was cool under the leaves; the sun was welding gaps in the canopy. I felt like breaking into a run. I kept walking, crossing fields, following hedgerows and tried not to dwell on the forthcoming second interview with the police. A couple of pheasants leapt noisily out of my way. I lost track of time, not caring I was late for lunch. Passing through a gate, I found myself only a hundred yards from The Three Bells. It seemed the nearest thing to an escape. As I pushed open the door, the first person I saw was Janette.

The second interview took place that afternoon. Three police officers were present. They seemed very formal.

She realised straight away that I was seriously troubled. At first I said it was the circumstances; that, like everyone else, I was bound to be upset. She knew me better than that. It wasn't only my sopping shoes that told on me; my hands were shaking. After we'd drunk two quick rounds, Janette persuaded me to tell her everything. I was in no state to resist; it was a relief to allow the events of the previous night to pour out. She listened in silence, then instructed me to remain sitting where I was. She seemed in complete control as she ordered more drinks and brought them back to the table. She asked me to pass her handbag, so I picked it up off the floor. She told me to open it and find her purse. I didn't bother to argue; I simply obeyed.

I inquired again how Andrea was. They assured me she was improving, but could not yet receive visitors. They asked whether I was aware of the nature of the girls' regulation night-attire.

I rummaged through odds and ends, but couldn't find her purse. She told me to try again. I was about to lose patience when, rifling, I found a small bottle of perfume in my hand.

They particularly wondered why Andrea had not been wearing her night-dress. They wanted to know why she was in only a dressing gown.

I stared at the bottle, then at Janette.

I said I had no idea.

For a minute, I was incapable of saying anything. When the minute was up, there was nothing to say.

They conferred briefly, then asked me if there was anything I ought to tell them. I decided there was.

My eyes couldn't leave her. She smiled and waited.

I said I had something to admit: Janette and I were lovers. I corrected myself and said that to call us lovers was more wish-fulfilment than truth. We had a relationship. Janette had visited my room that night.

The background noises of the pub had gone; so great was my concentration on Janette, I heard and saw nothing else. She faced me, her expression calm, her slender, uniformed figure relaxed. Last night taunted me. She watched me think.

The police left me alone for a few minutes. When they returned, one of them said it was not necessary to press me for details. They understood the situation, but explained it had been their duty to find out. I was asked whether Andrea had spoken to me about a sixth-former named Derek Thomas. I recalled she had mentioned the boy, but only in passing. I had heard some of Andrea's friends taunting her about being interested in him. His dormitory was on the third floor.

> I had to hear her say it; I needed it put into words. While I downed my drink like a man reprieved, Janette told me about 'Nightfall'. She'd been given two bottles as a gift a few days before. She'd opened one outside sickbay, sniffed it and hadn't been too keen. Andrea, who'd been to sickbay for skin cream, showed interest and asked to try some on her wrist. She liked it. Janette made her a present of the opened bottle, leaving the other one in her bag. Deliverance is too mild a word for what I felt. We walked back to school together in silence. There was nothing uncomfortable about it; I simply needed time to adjust. We kissed briefly as we parted and, while we faced each other, I tried to imagine making love to her. I wondered how necessary the loved one was; I even wondered whether the image alone could suffice. Without a word, we knew we'd often be together from then on. I imagined the darkness and her anonymity, and it worried me. Among the many sensations I experienced, I can't deny that the strongest was relief that I could face the next interview with the police.

They were satisfied with my explanation. The hospital was optimistic that Andrea would be discharged quite soon. The police apologised for probing into my personal life, but assumed I understood. They indicated they did not expect to be involved much longer; teenage love affairs were not their concern.

> Andrea was soon back at school. She was a celebrity for a while. She denied any involvement with Derek Thomas – much to his apparent relief – and ascribed her behaviour and fall to a bout of dizzy sickness. No longer class monitor,

she watches me from behind her desk, her bare arms resting on its top, and seems to smile reassuringly sometimes. It was two nights later, sitting in The Three Bells, that Janette asked me why I'd fallen silent. I remember I was frowning. Slowly, I picked up her handbag and opened it. I was already beginning to shake as realisation struggled through the confusion. The bottle of perfume rested in the palm of my hand. I knew, even before looking, that the seal hadn't been broken.

I was allowed to leave.

Not Writing Exactly

Well Id always wanted to be a writer and I knew I had the qualifications because I live in a Welsh mining village and Im on the dole and the game and Ive no idea about grammar and punctuation and my dad broke both my arms when I was a kid then sexually abused me for ten years and Im sitting here eating a macdonalds with my five kids who are bawling and one of them being sick on the shopping which Ive just bought with my giro and the cheque I received from the New Welsh Review for my latest short story.

It was when I was expecting Debbie whos my fourth that I took up shoplifting to make ends meet and go to the dance with Ann whos my friend and pushed drugs for Herbie until he got knifed by a boy who was always nice until he lost his reason one night because he tried drugs for the first time. Well we didnt pick anyone up but we had a great time and not many people were fighting and having glasses smashed in their faces and then Ann said to me why dont we break into old Mrs. Jenkins house and hang her up by her ankles and set fire to her cat. This sounded like a lot of fun but no I said because for one thing shes not English and for another thing she hasn't got any money.

So I only stood guard and thats how I got to court and put on probation and the judge said I was lucky I wasnt in gaol but he understood Id had a hard time and needed a break and anyway he didnt like old Mrs. Jenkins much either. It was my probation officer who changed my life and said I should write about my experiences and take a degree and then I got my MA but was surprised when he said write it honestly or itll sound like a parody. A parody I asked whats that and he told me and I was determined to learn about punctuation and all that. I began using full stops. Lots of them. Everywhere. And then, commas too, of which, I became inordinately proud, along with my, vocabulary. I impressed all my friend's by employing apostrophe's, which enhanced my abilities' to communicate what I couldn't express' before. I was so competent, so my probation officer opined, that I could apply to teach creative writing course's at Cardiff Universitys' course's for budding author's.

The prestigious appointment mine, I took up the post with fervid alacrity. What fun I had, jousting with words in tropes that pierced the foot, images sent sprawling, and I was no longer in danger of being slighted as that epitome of the oxymoron, the Welsh intellectual.

The euphoria couldn't last, of course. My work began to be rejected. I realised my life was at a literary low when even 'The New Welsh Review' returned a short story. Pensive, absentmindedly fingering the half-forgotten scars on my arms, I began to understand how far I'd strayed from my literary roots. Besides, the payments on my Porche were overdue.

So of course the only thing to do was what Ann and my probation officer who had got off with her said while they were at it in the back seat of my car and that was to be really genuine and spontaneous and write from the groin about how hard done by I am because of being educated when I could have been content left alone in the valley and completely stupid instead of a teacher and a brilliant writer in the ugliest of all fashionable styles.

Catchy Numbers

Anton Bruckner
The Lodge
Vienna
1st. November 1894

My dearest Liesl,

I don't understand what you mean. Eccentric? One, two, three. How can you call your dear Anton eccentric? One. One, two three, four. I love you. It's just that I like counting things – there's another one: five. And, dearest, you mustn't say I'm too old for you, or that you're too young for me, or that we're too young for both of us. Six, seven, eight. Love should always be unusual – eccentric, if you like – for who would ever want love to be ordinary, banal, commonplace? No, nobody would want that – there goes a ninth (or have I counted that one already?). Ten. My music is all yours – all nine symphonies, and number nought, so nine plus nought equals ten. Who has been turning you against me? Eleven, twelve. You can't really mean someone told you I'm a crank. I love you. Thirteen, fourteen, fifteen. A crank? Just because you're sixteen? Sometimes I think that you, like other people, don't understand me or my music or anything. Our age difference isn't so great; I'm only seventy. Seventy-one, seventy-two.

Why do you say my music is mathematical? I don't understand. A couple of my friends, three, four, say it's architectural – spacious even. Great cathedrals of sound. It's true those friends often ask me to alter my music – well, to cut it; but not by more than an hour or so in each symphony. And I studied so carefully; I didn't begin my fortieth symphony until I was one – or does that make me backward? You told me I'm gauche and look odd in my oversize collar and short, baggy trousers, but my trousers are the practical trousers of a true organist. You say people laugh at me.

What can one do? One can become two – me and you. One, two, me and you.

Dearest, we could marry and be secure. Don't reject me. It's so lonely living in this lodge with only a housekeeper for company. I'm honest and sincere. I'm a devout Roman Catholic and I believe in the Trinity, quartet, quintet, sestet. When I was organist in Linz Cathedral, I imagined my notes flying up among the beams and finding their way through the roof, then into the sky and heavenwards. I can get very close to God through my music; unfortunately, as you pointed out, my music doesn't get me very close to people – particularly the entire audience that walked out of one of my symphonies. Twenty-three, twenty-four. But my dear, you mustn't accuse me of being rustic and poorly educated. After all, I can count. Besides, I learned an enormous amount, quantity, quotient, tally, by studying the works of Mozart, Beethoven etc. I have diplomas and certificates, and I earn a considerable salary teaching at the Vienna Conservatory – more than enough, that is, for us to live on. We'd make a beautiful pair, triplet. And you'd bring forth, eventually, additions which would increase the sum of our happiness.

So, dearest, I beg you to stop counterpointing my optimism with your faint doubt – as when I first asked you to marry me and you coyly answered, 'You must be joking!' I care for you and understand you. Of course I do. You're a little uncertain, in the same way my critics are sometimes; as when my second symphony was called 'nonsense' and my third 'unperformable'. And so forth, fifth, sixth.

Part of the reason for my rejection is Wagner, whom the Viennese hate. My dear, do you realise I actually met him? I really spoke to him. At our first meeting, I fell on my knees in front of him and, of course, I never sat in his presence. You can imagine how overawed I was. I'd taken a few of my scores with me (so how many's that?) and I asked whether I could dedicate one to him. He actually agreed! And then we went for a few beers, and a few more, and how many that was I'll never know. The trouble was, I also couldn't remember which symphony I'd dedicated to him.

I wish I could compose as well as Wagner did. I have an idea or two, or more, for a love song that will sum up my feelings for you. It would be as concise as all my work; i.e. endless, like our love. Initially, before I met you, my first concern was music, but that became tertiary as you became secondary; then you were the prime mover who would make me whole, steady and even, instead of, as you said, 'unbelievably odd'.

Darling, you are my tonic, sub-dominant, my only one. Your attributes are countless, legion, numberless. I dream naughty dreams and think treble entendres about you, your statistics beyond measure, vital, an unknown quantity I shall never have enough of. You're my music, my crotchet, my quaver, semi-quaver, demisemiquaver, hemisemidemihemisemiquaver. With you, I lose count; without you I'm solo. My nervous breakdown and the sanatorium are in the past; I have found my heavenly symphony. I love your performance, your rhythm, your parts, your movements. I thrill to your vibratos, passages and variations. And they say there's no eroticism in my work. You're my grace note, my duet, and my perfect forth. My tutti.

Please, my dear, next time I call, don't emulate the public and walk out, especially before I begin my overture. I'll be great one day, you'll see. Do you know, I received a fifteen-minute ovation after my seventh symphony? I cried. I couldn't help it. Is that eccentric? Fifteen and seven. Maybe my music will be remembered. Maybe each performance won't be a one-off. Take pity on a singular, besotted old man. Seventy-one, seventy-two. Years are frightening things, but who's counting?

Your loving double, your counterpart, your adoring but lonely,

Anton.

Loudmouth

I despised him. We all did. Like the rest of the pub crowd, I accepted his drinks, but only bought him one back when I had to. He never took the hint. One or two of us laughed openly at him, but he was so thick-skinned, so full of himself, he didn't seem to notice.

One Wednesday evening he came into the pub at his usual time – his name's Glyn, by the way. I had my back to the door, but Martin groaned, so I knew very well who had entered. Within a minute, Glyn was dominating the conversation, expatiating (such a bulbous word, but it fit him) on the expensive meal he'd bought his wife the previous night. We had to go through each course, mouthful by mouthful; we were told the price of each dish; we listened to his pseudo- connoisseur's judgement of the wine and we were given an I-spy description of the décor. It wasn't just that he bored us; it was the *way* he bored us that rankled. He stored impressive, pompous phrases just so he could use them at times like this. He rummaged through them like a fanatic at a jumble sale, leaving nothing untried. Out came 'sybaritic', 'sumptuous repast' and 'otiose'. 'Epicurean' was tried for size, found too small and discarded for 'hedonistic'. The larger the word, the more likely it was to elbow its way to the front. He regaled us – he's got *me* at it now – he told us about his wife's finery, how he'd instructed the waiter on the best way to serve vegetables and how he'd sent back their bottle of wine ('It was corked, you know – I never accept a sub-standard bottle of wine'). Of course, the head waiter addressed him by his first name, and these outings were always paid for with a Diners' Card ('Not available to just anyone, you know'). The joke was – and everyone was aware of it – we knew he was lying through his teeth.

Martin had discovered, quite accidentally, that Glyn drove a mini-cab on Tuesday and Thursday evenings. A few words with another driver had confirmed it. Ever since Glyn had blustered his way into our company about three months previously, we'd been treated to a detailed description of his Very Important Job. It was a high-powered accountancy position with a multi-national. Except that it wasn't. Martin had phoned one day, just for the hell of it, and discovered Glyn was little more than a clerk. If it wasn't his job, it was his house; he regularly gave us earache about the D.I.Y. improvements he was continually making. He had 'multifarious abilities he could turn his hand to, on occasion' and this, no doubt, was why his house would soon be worth twice what he paid for it. But the worst was his wife.

His wife. She was Venus incarnate. She was Delia Smith, Florence Nightingale and Helen of Troy all rolled into one. Well, it made a change, I suppose, to hear someone actually praising his wife. When Martin dropped the photograph of her into his beer – accidentally, of course – Glyn didn't flinch; he seemed to have an endless supply.

Granted, she was striking – beautiful even. If it *was* his wife. You see, none of us had ever clapped eyes on her – not in the flesh. For all we knew, Glyn could have been a bachelor. Not once – not even on a Saturday night – had he brought her to the pub. Martin was convinced she was too good to be true, that the photographs were of someone else entirely. I was inclined to agree. I couldn't imagine such a woman falling for a windbag like Glyn. Sometimes we asked him why he never brought her along and his excuses became a standing joke. 'Fancy her Mother turning up from Dorset like that,' or, 'We were just leaving the house when she gashed her finger and insisted I go on alone,' and wilder explanations that had us grinning into our beer. We began to vie with each other to see who could produce the most ludicrous excuse. Sometimes, when Glyn arrived, *he* won.

But this particular Wednesday was different. It began normally enough; Glyn swaggered in, bought the next two rounds, then launched into a monologue so dull it had the paper peeling from the walls. I don't remember all of it – something about his competence and how easy it is to be rich. In passing, Martin asked him whether he'd come by cab, but the dig was lost on Glyn. Some of our crowd simply turned away and played darts. Martin and I tried to edge him out of the remaining circle but, no matter which way I turned, he popped up like one of those recurring dreams. I remember some of his phrases: 'prodigious responsibilities', 'emblematic handshakes' and even 'a tangible estimation of assiduity'. His wife, needless to say, wasn't required to work, despite being a qualified teacher and an experienced secretary. Helen apparently, had no need to grace the world with her manifold talents (you see how catching it is?). I was almost glad when it was time to go home.

However (nevertheless, indeed, notwithstanding) what happened next was totally unexpected. Glyn wrapped himself in his Saville Row overcoat (which, strangely enough, was displayed in every Burton shop window), wished (desired, bade) us all a 'serene and starry goodnight' and set off for his D.I.Y.-improved Troy. The door had hardly closed behind him when we heard a sickening squeal of tyres.

Now, as you've no doubt gathered, Martin and I weren't exactly Glyn's best friends; but we didn't wish him run over. Fearing the worst, we ran outside, half-expecting to see him sprawled in the road. He ushered us aside.

He was in his element. He helped control the traffic, then threw his overcoat over the casualty, who was lying at the side of the road. A middle-aged woman – evidently the driver of the car involved – was sobbing nearby. Luckily, a young constable was soon on hand, but Glyn, with scant regard for the bobby's authority, appropriated (all right, took) his personal R/T and ordered the surprised voice on the other end to call an ambulance. It was soon clear that the figure lying in the road had a broken leg. I flinched as I suddenly realized Glyn was about to put it in a splint. I'm sure I was no less relieved than the casualty when the policeman reasserted his authority and took charge.

When the ambulance arrived, Glyn thought it necessary to offer the experts the benefit of his advice – so much so that one of them exhibited something less than a bedside manner. That didn't stop Glyn insisting on accompanying the casualty to hospital; even the casualty's objections couldn't prevent that. Martin and I (in our defence, let me remind you we'd been drinking all night) decided it was our duty to our drinking-partner to explain to Helen what had delayed her Paris. As Glyn clambered into the ambulance, we giggled at the prospect of exposing one of his big lies.

We parked, slightly askew, outside a Victorian semi. It was the first time we'd seen Glyn's house and our first reaction was that it looked a bit scruffy. We were delighted. The window panes were wooden and partially rotted, the brickwork badly needed re-pointing and, from what we could see of the roof, it was clear some slates were cracked and others missing. We managed to stop giggling before we rang the bell. A voice from somewhere inside the house called, 'Come in – it's not locked,' and, keen to meet Glyn's paragon of virtue and loveliness, we pushed open the door.

The hallway was dim and dingy. We shuffled towards the light of a half-open door. It was clear straight away that Glyn hadn't lied about doing work on the house, but there was no sign of plastering or decorating. Only rails. And steps had been converted to slopes. We entered the room and came face to face with the original of Glyn's photographs.

Helen – the Helen we recognized, only much older – faced us from her wheelchair. She'd been beautiful once, but now she looked like a crumpled photograph of herself, the skin of her face and hands creased, a rug half-covering her once-shapely legs. Neither Martin nor I could speak. She apologized for the state of the house. She explained that the Social Security people were doing their best, but that Glyn wasn't prepared to sit around and wait. He intended, she said, to earn enough from his job and his cabbing to complete the important modifications soon. The decorating would have to wait.

Martin and I had sobered instantly. We didn't have to be told; we knew multiple sclerosis when we saw it. She listened to our subdued explanation of why Glyn would be late home. She nodded slowly, clearly understanding a lot more than we said. I wanted to get out, but we had no choice except to stay a few minutes. During this time, it became clear that Glyn had married her after she'd been confined to a wheelchair. She wasn't able to get out much, most of her excursions being to the hospital and the clinic. I glanced towards the few books on the shelves, an old radio by a divan, pairs of old-fashioned shoes under a chair.

She told us she used to be a teacher. She'd loved the work and enjoyed the sound of children playing. There was a school not far away and, every weekday, she could hear the shouts and calls from its playground. When she'd had to give up teaching, she'd qualified as a secretary, but then even a desk job became too much and now she occupied herself at home as best she could. We asked if there was anything she needed. There wasn't. We offered to do whatever Glyn would have done, had he been there. There was nothing. Martin and I left the house and drove back in silence.

Two nights later, Glyn came into the pub. He seemed his usual self. Martin and I weren't sure whether to refer to what had happened – we were sure Helen must have mentioned our visit. If so, Glyn had decided not to allude to it. He talked about the accident and how the casualty wasn't too badly hurt, but not a word about what had happened afterwards. Finally, Martin and I made a decision. We took Glyn aside and hesitantly asked whether we could help with his home repairs. I wasn't sure how he would take it, whether we were doing the right thing. At first, he seemed a bit defensive, but then he relaxed, accepted, and began to talk to us as friends, and in simple, unaffected language.

I'm pleased to say Glyn now brings Helen to the pub every Saturday night. She looks forward to it and it's good to see how much she talks and smiles. Glyn finds it unnecessary to take centre stage and, although the occasional pompous phrase still slips out sometimes, it really doesn't matter and, anyway, he doesn't buttonhole people the way he used to. We all welcome him when he comes in and I'm sure, nowadays, he drinks more pints than he buys. And I, for one, spend a great deal more time listening to him.

Escalation

Dear Field Marshal Llewelyn,

I write this letter in the hope of mitigating the recent unpleasantness between us. The prison guards have been kind enough to supply me with pen and paper, so I'll set down my position clearly. I want you to be in possession of all the facts before my public trial takes place. Perhaps, when you learn of my extenuating circumstances, you'll take a more understanding view of what happened.

First, I insist that only *four* giraffes were involved, not the seven specified in the charges. Secondly – and I'd have thought that you, of all people, would have known this – the Panzer Kraftwagen Mark Four tank does *not* have lights fitted as standard equipment. Neither, I need hardly add, did it have them during the Second World War. I do, however, concede that the avalanche that blocked the A4069 might be construed, by some, as my responsibility. But the damage to Brynamman I must lay at nobody's door but your own. By the way, the train which got bogged down on Brecon Beacons was not of the type that runs on rails (as the charges, ludicrously, seem to imply) but an old-style wagon train. Which, of course, accounts for the Red Indians.

So much for the preliminary minor points. I feel constrained to tell you, Field Marshal Llewelyn, that I find your description of events that night somewhat confusing. I trust this letter is clarifying the situation.

I'll begin at eleven p.m. on the night in question. I was sitting on a rock at the summit of Garreg- Lwyd. I was dressed as Wild Bill Hickok and cleaning my rifle by lamplight. So far then, everything was perfectly normal.

You can imagine my surprise when I was informed the paratroops would be late. Despite the rain, I could see the Big Top pitched on a slope in the valley. My first thought was to get on the radio and inform the circus, but I couldn't get through. It later transpired that their wireless operator had inadvertently tuned in to S4C and gone into a coma.

I can understand that you think, at this point, my response was ill-judged. But, I sincerely ask you, what could I do? What would you do in the same situation? I just did what any sensible person would do in the same circumstances; I buckled on my six-guns and ran screaming and shooting down the hillside.

Unfortunately, maybe due to the rain, my action was misconstrued by the circus people. Instead of delaying the start, they carried on according to schedule: the floodlights went on and the wagon train sped out of the Big Top. However, instead of racing across the Beacons and forming a circle, it drove straight into a marsh and got stuck.

Even then the problem might have been rectified if it hadn't been for Big Chief Prancing Sheep. It must have been obvious, even to him, that something was wrong; but still he led his braves into the attack on the wagon train. There was no choice but to carry on. The cameras were rolling and I could hear the drone of the aeroplane overhead. I could only hope Big Chief Prancing Sheep would realise what had happened and prolong his attack. Fat chance! Instead of prancing about whooping and waving his chopper, he made straight for the cowboys. Consequently, I shot him on the spot.

You might think I was at fault here. I maintain he forced me to kill him ahead of schedule and, if I were at liberty, I'd sue him for breach of contract. I'd never have employed the feathered fool if the agency hadn't insisted on his Welsh ancestry. It doesn't surprise me.

Meanwhile, I had worse problems to worry about. According to the script, the circus was supposed to be caught up in the Normandy landings of nineteen forty-four. Jim Splicer, the Commander of the Panzer Kraftwagen Mark Four tanks – who is, I'm pleased to hear, making satisfactory progress in Amman Valley Hospital – was supposed to be moving his armour up the A4069 to a nearby ridge. When I focused my binoculars on him, I wasn't too pleased to see he'd been waved down by a Panda car. I found out later that the Welsh Constabulary hadn't, as I suspected, stopped the tanks because they were destroying the A4069; it was a routine check for bald tyres. And every tank was booked for driving without lights.

Which brings me, Field Marshal, to the main bone of contention between us. I had *no idea* the British Army – or what used to be the British Army – was holding manoeuvres that night. When your men stormed over the ridge, my circus people naturally assumed they were part of Jim Splicer's German force. So, in accordance with the script, the clowns, cowboys and acrobats mounted an attack upon your men. As part of the cinematic spectacle, the animals were let loose.

I'd like, at this point, to apologise about the Welch Fusilier being eaten by lions. *My* soldiers, I might add, were suitably padded. Perhaps this lesson might prove beneficial when you plan your next war.

Before I move on to the more serious aspects of this night, one small point: it's not my fault one of your tanks fired at one of mine. Nor that the particular tank fired at was made of rubber. The fatal consequences of the rebound must be attributed to a power far greater than mine. Furthermore, I suggest the flame-thrower attack was an act of sheer pique. I doubt whether you appreciate the cost of rubber tanks. I understand the National Trust is eager to learn when the solidified puddle will be removed – especially as, at the last count, five frolicking lambs have trampolined to their deaths on it. They await your proposals. Not to mention the animals.

Had Big Chief Prancing Sheep not stood up at this moment, I might have maintained my usual equilibrium. In full shot, a bullet hole in his heart, he jumped up and regaled his braves with a story about my alleged mistreatment of him – a sort of 'one more breach in the contract, dear friends'. As a result, his war party attacked the camera crew. The whole thing was beginning to look like something by Hieronymous Bosch.

I admit that the arrival of my paratroops further confused an already muddled situation. Those of them who pressed home their attack, despite landing on the backs of giraffes, were only showing a commendable zeal so often lacking in crowd scenes. The clowns, cowboys and contortionists, led by me, six-guns blazing, made for a hillock beside what was left of the A4069. This hillock, as shown clearly in the love-scene shot the previous day between me and Miss Myrtle Tydfil, was ideally suited to the setting of a heroic last stand against the Germans. I concede that the script might not have measured up to the standards of Greek tragedy, but then Garreg-Lwyd is hardly Parnassus. Besides, Aeschylus didn't have Big Chief Prancing Sheep for one of his characters. Not to mention the animals.

The idea was, not unreasonably, that the circus cowboys had prepared for an Indian uprising, but now led the fight for Normandy. The circus people, with full supporting cast, were supposed to struggle desperately for many long and hard hours against Jim Splicer's Panzers. Unwittingly, they found themselves fighting a crack force of the modern British Army. I'd like to ask you, Field Marshal, how, if they weren't supposed to be able to beat a largely rubberised tank battalion in under six hours, they beat *your* ultra-modern armour in ten minutes flat. And with bows and arrows. It's hardly surprising that questions were asked in the House – or would have been, had events not taken a turn for the worse.

Incidentally, Miss Myrtle Tydfil might have the reputation of a man-eating prima donna, but your claim she raped six Welch Fusiliers is, I suggest, exaggerated. Even the police put the number at only four.

Also, no modern cinema audience would be surprised when my Seventh Cavalry pounded over the hill to our rescue. However, *they* were mildly surprised, to say the least, when you blew them off the Beacons with your heavy field guns. Not to mention the animals.

Which brings me to the avalanche. It's my contention that I showed great presence of mind. In his haste to run away, one of your men left his lorry with its handbrake unapplied. As you'll be aware, the lorry to which I refer is the one that was loaded with landmines.

The lorry began rolling towards Brynamman. Without a thought for my own safety, I put on a fire-proof, anti-flash outfit, a bullet-resistant jacket, chemically-filtered breathing apparatus and my shock-proof watch. I jumped into an armour-clad personnel carrier and, waiting only for the camera crews to set up their equipment, raced after the lorry.

When the lorry exploded, widening the Amman Valley by a hundred yards or so, Brynamman Rugby Club was celebrating the day's win, so nobody heard the fifty tons of landmines go off. But, when the drinkers left the club, they couldn't help noticing Brynamman was missing. When they questioned me about this, I said I didn't recollect seeing any such place. Considering they'd climbed over its rubble to ask me, I suspected my little ruse wouldn't stand up to careful scrutiny. So I hit on an idea.

This is when the trouble started. Showing remarkable calm, I informed my listeners that the day of the glorious rising had arrived – that I was the Commander of the Welsh National Liberation Army. They took one look at my Wild Bill Hickok outfit and believed me. (As you're aware, charge number ninety-eight accuses me of impersonating an officer of Plaid Cymru.)

As soon as word got round Wales – which, I swear, took no longer than five minutes – I found myself at the head of a beery, daffodil-wielding rabble, which, singing 'The Battle Hymn of the Republic', stormed the Severn Bridge. The rest, as they say, is history.

Field Marshal – or should I say 'President' now? – I beg you not to go ahead with my show trial. At least, not in Welsh. I sympathise with your motives, particularly in the light of the recent unlawful repainting of road signs into English in London, but surely a show of mercy would reveal you as a benevolent ruler? If you set me free, I promise never to mention my own inadvertent part in your glorious accession to power. (Who'd have expected the Severn Bridge toll booths to be on strike?)

Assuring you of my constant and devoted fealty at all times,

Yours faithfully,

Neal Mason.

P.S. Good luck with the Welsh space programme. The rugby-ball-shaped satellite is a stroke of genius.

Letter to the Editor

Dear Editor,

Being a journalist, precision is my prime concern. And celebration. Also accuracy and clarity without diversions and excuses. And logic. So, straight to my point – not forgetting grammar. And memory. But does this poem have them? Surely, of all the arts, poetry is the most precise, the most compact and sincere. The most memorable. Yet what do we have here? Muddle. Rhetoric. Have you ever read a more garbled poem?

(Perhaps not. But having, as yet, not the faintest idea which poem is referred to, I reserve judgement. Ed.)

Look at its style. Being myself a stylist, I personally consider the whole tenor of the poem, that is to say, the drift and underlying direction, an assertion addressed to a female, if argument there be – for the reasoning is impossible to follow – a declaration while being indirect, without such indirectness being complimentary to, or even essential to, the subject and theme.

(The Pisan Cantos? Ed.)

And the first line, comprising, as it does, of five syllables –

(A haiku? Ed.)

–unless you count the other ten, leads one to expect, or demand, greater acuity and cohesion. It promises faithfulness and eternity, but are the promises fulfilled? Can the proffered love be trusted? My feminine sensibility was touched, yet I feared it might be betrayed. I was struck by the resonance of the fifth word of the eighteenth line, which I quote here in full:

the

However, on re-reading, I realised I had been misled. Here was no reference, as I naturally thought, to the first syllable of theology, or therapy, or thermodynamic equilibrium; the poet had merely meant the definite article. Talk about banal. Are we seriously supposed to accord this work the status of a potential classic? And that's another thing.

(What is? Ed.)

This poem's writer, or perpetrator, clearly knows nothing about love or sunlight on trees or appealing fluffy animals, not to mention meadows covered with ordure.

(Verdure, surely? Ed.)

Imagine for a moment that poetry is art.

(Difficult, but I'll try. Ed)

I suggest, in my reticent, humble opinion, that this poem is crap.

(Cancel verdure. Ed.)

There's about as much art in this poem as there is comedy at the Edinburgh Fringe. What about marriage? And vows of eternal union? 'Epithalamium' he calls it. This is to wed promises with lies, intentions with amnesia. Like all journalists, I value clarity and truth. So I must say there are things to be said in favour of this poem and in favour of being critical of it. The best part of the poem is, to be precise, no worse, in its better phases, than the best a poor poet can aspire to, and it has, perhaps, never been bettered by a worse poet. Some poems, even though worse, are, in parts, better than this, and this is better than being worse than a better poet at his worst. The minor elements I can't understand are only the syntax, form, images, metaphors and form. The rest is clear.

(Makes sense. More sense than Leavis anyway. Ed.)

But this is where things get difficult. On top of the obscurity, it's the deceit. Why should this be?

(I'm frightened to ask. Ed.)

Grammar mixed with a false style. You're right to question it and so am I because I'm a journalist and care deeply about language, this poem being, as they are, adulterated, which is about the best one can say of it, all else being equal at the end of the day. When we scanned the words, is it a good metre, or have the meaning been ill-stressed? To easily split hairs on this point is very unique to illustrate, given this poet's expressions like peas in a pod. So it's obvious this poem is incompetent and insincere right from the first line which promises, 'Memory shall flower, our anniversary fresh'.

(Hang on a moment – that's *my* poem! Ed.)

And goes on to the last line: 'squelching in squeaky boots through polished winter', which is so inept as to be frightening.

(You bitch! Ed.)

In conclusion, I'd like to nominate this poem, 'Epithalamium', for the McGonagall Memorial Trophy.

(That's quite enough of that! Ed.)

Ed, will you please stop interrupting!

(Who's the bloody Editor here? Ed.)

I haven't finished making my case.

(Look, just because I forgot our anniversary –)

'Memory shall flower, our anniversary fresh'. Ed, you didn't even buy me a card!

(I did – almost. What with the pressure of work and all these bloody readers' letters, I forgot. Ed.)

Your own wife. Not even a card.

(Look, don't cry. I'll make it up to you.)

You called me a bitch.

(I'm sorry, really I am. Look, I'll take you out to dinner to help make up for it. O.K.?)

I don't know. I'm too upset.

(Anywhere you like.)

The Ritz?

(Er…)

You don't love me! You've never loved me!

(All right, all right, the Ritz.)

You promise?

(I promise. Now, finish your letter, otherwise I'll have to work late.)

All right. In conclusion, I suggest this poet shows promise which needs encouraging. It's only his lack of empathy – that's to say, consideration – that lets him, and others, down. His celebration of the past, despite loss of memory, lacks only a sense of occasion. However, his evocation of food, especially dinner, helps mitigate his failings – it would, though, sound more poetic if accompanied by a description of nature; an enormous bunch of flowers, for instance.

Yours sincerely,

Eileen.

P.S. Meet you there at seven. Don't be late.

Late Delivery

Dear Jenny,

If it were to anyone else, I'd baulk at the shock this letter will bring – after all, how many widows receive a letter from their dead husband? But, in this case, circumstances are different, aren't they?

If my solicitor is as efficient as usual, today it's exactly one month since my death. No doubt you're tearfully re-running how your beloved husband was killed. I visualise you weeping quietly with the curtains drawn, a treasured photograph clutched to your breast, vows of eternal love on your trembling lips.

So much for fantasy. If the curtains are drawn, it's because you've got a man clutched to your breasts, a glass of gin near your lips. You're not the type to weep; if someone upsets you, it's not tears you let fall, but crockery and glassware.

I know you too well, Jenny. The existence of this letter proves it. The man clutched to your breast is Malcolm – like you, a born plotter. I'm aware of some of the tactics he used to build up his firm of electrical contractors, his operations covering half the county, including our bedroom. The fights between you two and me were ugly, but I didn't take your threats seriously – not until you stopped making them. Then I knew you really would try to kill me.

Evidently you succeeded, otherwise you wouldn't be reading this. I've been vigilant, of course, but it's not possible to check everything. Besides, I suspect the means you've employed are electrical and I can't compete with Malcolm's knowledge in that area. I took precautions, although it soon struck me that certain precautions had been taking themselves.

Among your insults and recriminations, one topic came up time and again. Right from the start of our marriage, you accused me of keeping something from you. I regularly disappeared for a few hours every week. These absences grew in your mind and, you being you, it had to be a lover. In turn, I accused you of marrying a meal ticket. Marriage is difficult at the best of times; it's even harder when the husband is so much older than the woman.

It's possible, I suppose, that the police suspect foul play. You could be reading this in prison. But, as I say, I know you too well; you're a manipulator. You've got Malcolm to do the dirty work and, if anything goes wrong, you'll be the ignorant, innocent bystander. I'd bet my life on it, so to speak.

This letter is the explanation I never gave you. At first, I kept my secret to spare you anguish – at least, that's how I convinced myself. I loved you. With hindsight, maybe I hid a feeling of shame and guilt. Anyway, it crossed my mind you took up with Malcolm as revenge – until, that is, I found out you'd been around with him before our marriage. Not only that but, no matter what he thought, he wasn't the only one with visiting rights. Yet there were times when you could be kindness itself. Remember our holiday in the Lake District? When, on the first day, I twisted my ankle, the holiday seemed to be ruined. But you took over the driving and refused to let anything spoil those perfect July days.

I suppose we're too cynical to believe such memories can be taken to the grave. My first wife – who, as you know, died many years ago, and to whom you couldn't hold a candle – thought otherwise. Unlike me, she was a regular church-goer, a considerate and gentle person. And I didn't love her. You, of course, are slovenly, self-centred and soulless. And I loved you – still would, if it was possible.

I told you my first wife died in an accident. That's not the whole truth. I told you we'd had no children. That also wasn't the whole truth.

She gave birth a year after we were married. A son. It was a difficult birth, but the difficulties were only just beginning. We christened him Drew. He was a strange child. He brooded continually and laughed far less frequently than other children. He seemed, with one exception, emotionally detached. He was capable of great cruelty, especially to pets we hoped he'd learn to care for. Although not unintelligent, he was virtually unteachable. We had to send him to a special school. One particular facet of his personality was especially feared by those at his school. It wasn't only that he could inflict injury; he could harbour a grudge for ages and took pleasure in planning a thorough revenge.

I said there was one exception to his emotional detachment. In all the world, and for no obvious reason, there was only one person he was devoted to, a person he regarded as beyond criticism or fault. Me.

The psychiatrists tried to exploit this positive trait by widening his focus. They thought, as Drew was so attached to me, he might grow to care for the people and things I cared for.

He was allowed home at weekends. On one of these visits – it was a month before Drew was fifteen – my wife and I had a serious disagreement. The resident Doctor at Drew's school had told us he thought Drew should be committed to a closed institution. My wife, reluctantly, felt the Doctor was right. I argued that it would amount to a full stop in Drew's life, an admission of defeat. We got heated. While pronouncing Drew a danger to society, my wife's eyes suddenly focused somewhere behind me. I turned to look. Drew was standing motionless in the doorway. We couldn't tell how long he'd been there, but his stillness, his fixed expression and unblinking eyes, suggested he'd heard a great deal.

It took a year and a week. Drew hadn't been put into a closed institution – largely thanks to me – and was home one hot weekend in August. My wife was in our swimming pool, lazing on her back on an air-bed, one arm trailing in the water. Drew began mowing the lawn, the electric burr reaching me in the living-room. I looked through the window and saw he'd cut the edge-line perfectly straight. The second line too looked almost perfect. It was a sweltering day. But, when I glanced up again, I chilled. The third line was swerving way off course. The green trail, paler than the uncut grass, curved towards the pool. Some sixth sense alerted my wife. She propped herself up on the air-bed. The line of mown grass now straight, it pointed directly towards her. She shouted something. So did I. The mower was only a few yards from the edge when Drew let go. He stood still and watched the mower reach the pool, the mower's orange cable like a snake eager for water.

For a moment, it looked as though my wife's presence of mind might save her. She took her arm out of the water and spread her weight on the air-bed. But she was near the edge of the pool and the splash created a deadly wave.

It was a long time ago, Jenny, but that day is always with me. You accused me of seeing someone else and you were right; my son. All my disappearances were visits to him. So you see, I was never unfaithful to you. My fault was that I could never bring myself to tell you about Drew. Once or twice I came close, but something always happened to dissuade me.

So you've finally learned my secret. Drew, although adjudged criminally insane, was a minor at the time. On each of my visits over the years, he's been clarity itself and his attachment to me is stronger than ever. Of course, he's long been old enough for us to discuss everything – including, naturally, you. I told him every detail. I told him about your drinking. I told him about you and Malcolm. I told him about your threats. At this, I registered his stillness, his fixed expression, his unblinking eyes.

I'm sorry things didn't work out for us, Jenny. Enjoy the house and possessions and Malcolm. You can make plans. You can map your long-term future.

By the way, Drew was released a month ago. I've little doubt he's located my grave and repaid one of my visits. Well, there's nothing I can do now. It's all too late.

Goodbye Jenny. Sleep well.

With love and regret,

N.

Beauty and the Beast

Amman Valley Asylum
for Distressed Naturalists

The Welsh Geographic,
Scientific and Rare Species Society

Dear Committee,

It is with mixed feelings I submit this preliminary account of my recent expedition. I regard it as a great honour to address your learned and august Society; I only wish I was at liberty to present my findings personally and at inordinate length. Nevertheless, the specimens I sent you will, I am sure, provide you with invaluable information about the rare and, in one case at least, previously supposed – but now definitely – extinct species it was my privilege to tread on. But I trust tiny areas of the wings remain unsquashed and that, by scaling down the flattened areas, you can arrive at a very fair approximation of size.

First, allow me to express my sincere appreciation of your committee's decision to recognise my eminence in the field, long delayed though such recognition has been, and to fund this exciting and, I may say, dangerous project. The moment your cheque arrived – even though there was an error in the name and address – I hurried round to the co-op to purchase all the essential equipment, not forgetting climbing-gear, skis, breathing apparatus, fifteen tents and ten huskies.

At home, I studied my map of the proposed exploration area and decided that, because Brynamman borders such a hilly part of Brecon Beacons, it was incumbent upon me to select the safest possible Base Camp for my team. Hence my choice of the Derlwyn Arms on the main road.

I am, as you so correctly stated in your letter of engagement, despite your mistakes when referring to my CV, too experienced and too professional to take unnecessary risks. However, there was no concealing the tension as we staggered from the hostelry, feeling already the effects of reduced oxygen at seven hundred feet above sea level. The landlord could hardly contain the emotion in his voice as he enquired whether we would be back for the evening meal. I was obliged to inform him we might be gone for some time.

I led the way. I was under no illusions as to the nature of my responsibilities, nor the severity of the terrain, a full three hundred yards of which we had to traverse to Camp One. It is difficult to convey the thoughts and feelings of us pioneers on such occasions. What longings or misgivings we had, we kept to ourselves, the silence broken only by the rock music from Megan's earphone.

It was only after my careful selection of Megan that I decided to keep the number in my expedition small. And, limiting it to the two of us, how fortunate my choice proved to be. Although an undergraduate and with no knowledge of geography, science or botany (her degree course focusing on thirteenth-century Thai boxing manuscripts) she revealed, that night, a natural awareness of biology I can only describe as astonishing.

It had been my intention, of course, to return the fourteen superfluous tents to the suppliers, but this proved unnecessary; the single husky that survived the mass dog-fight had chewed them beyond recognition. To Megan's relief, I explained that huskies, not being an endangered species, survive in considerable numbers and, having no individuality, do not mind their slaughter at all, and probably welcome it.

Eating our goat's yoghurt breakfast early next morning, we gazed at a vista of barren beauty, the sun heating moss-softened rocks. Nowhere was there a sign of human habitation. There wasn't even a pub. It was eerie. The landscape was stark, its complete lack of trees reinforcing our sense of isolation. But, as Megan remarked, tuning in to pop music on Radio Wales and exhibiting acceptance and fortitude that were nothing less than inspiring, when you've seen one tree, you've seen them all.

We began the serious business of study and exploration. Aware of the danger from insects and their dislike of smoke, I lit one of the Full Corona Havana cigars so crucially provided from your funds. We collected specimens and began to record flora and fauna. It was while I was writing that, quite suddenly, the rarest of Welsh butterflies, Cymryg loppyflopus, leapt up in front of me. I could hardly believe my eyes. Buffeted by the breeze, it fluttered delicately above a patch of spurge. Agape, I watched its diaphanous, harp-shaped, red-and-green wings flit gracefully this way and that, rising and falling against a backdrop of light-blue sky until, finally, it settled on a lichen-covered boulder where, tired from her exertions, Megan sat on it.

With a squeal, she too leapt into the air. Concerned as I was for Loppyflopus, I was more alarmed about Megan's safety. The poison of this wonderful butterfly was, I knew, very strong and there wasn't a moment to lose. I bounded over the equipment. Reaching her, I tore down her jeans and sank my teeth into the affected area. I hoped I could extract the poison in time. Lying on the grass, Megan began to writhe and I was soon gratified to learn she definitely wasn't suffering.

It had been a narrow escape. With hindsight, so to speak, I realise it was an omen of far more hazardous events to come. Tucking Megan into her sleeping-bag, I told her to be brave while I fetched medical assistance. Then, alerted by a primitive instinct deep within me, I unpacked my rifle.

I had opted for the recoilless Megablaster Mark IV made by the Cardiff Arms Park factory. I loaded it with steel-jacketed bullets (smokeless, of course, my concern about pollution always my priority) and set off, totally alone. I carefully noted my compass bearing, the wind direction, the angle of the sun and the contours of the landscape. Then I raced towards the pub.

Oh fateful day. It's as though the storm had been waiting, deliberately hiding behind the two-thousand-foot summit of

Garreg Lwyd. The moment I was in the open, it pounced. It tore at my hands and feet, clawed at my face. Thrown off course, I staggered blindly through mist and rain. Then, unexpectedly, it cleared. The sky was blue again, the horizon shimmered. But my surroundings were unfamiliar. I was lost. And then I noticed the giant hoof-print.

Even as I gaped, I felt conscious of being watched. Above me, a pair of buzzards, virtually extinct in lowland Britain, circled like vultures. Noticing what appeared to be a dishevelled feather on one of them, and worried its hunting ability might be impaired, I shot it. Comparing it with its mate, which I also shot, I was greatly relieved to find my fear had been unfounded. Both birds were in wonderful condition and, alive, would have been in perfect health. Pleased I hadn't wasted the fifty shots, I admired the marvellous creatures.

However, I had more-important matters to consider – but, despite my cigars being soggy, I managed to light one. Pocketing the gold lighter so crucially provided by your funds, I examined the hoof-print.

Folk tales from Brynamman's pubs began to echo in my head. I witnessed again the terror in local inhabitants' eyes. The memory of their warnings induced a shiver. Blood-curdling screams at night. Horses eaten whole. Streams drunk dry. Could it possibly be – was this really the hoof-print of the Abominable Snowram?

Despite the sunshine, I felt cold. The fearful world of Celtic magic seemed uncomfortably close. Was I to be the next victim of the horrible man-eating sheep? I took out my silver hip-flask, so crucially provided by your funds, and drank.

I followed the hoof-prints. Had I not been so passionate about conservation and wildlife, my nerve might have failed me. As I followed the hoof-prints, I nearly fell into one; a fetid, primordial pong lingered in the bottom. I didn't dare imagine the size of the creature I was tracking. Sometimes it became difficult to distinguish its droppings from enormous boulders, the lumps of schist the largest I've ever seen.

I arrived at what must have been the beast's lair. I still wake up screaming. Eyes widening, I beheld a decomposing mattress and a rotting pram. Then the skeleton of an umbrella. Had the Abominable Snowram eaten people while they slept? Perhaps the umbrella owner had attempted a futile defence.

And yet, apart from such terrors, the place had great attraction and could have been a beauty spot. It was a valley, greened with ferns and tumbles of leaves. It had serenity. Pebbles rattled in a stream and sounded soothing and eternal.

Seduced, I began to admire unspoilt details. A graceful Plastic Bag fish, its Spar marking vivid in the water, was filter-feeding on a shoal of Dog-ends. Nearby, the Candied or Common cola, still young enough not to be camouflaged by its second winter's corrosion, displayed for a mate. I was thrilled to see it had achieved considerable success, having attracted a pile not far away. They were busy gobbling tiny frogs, all presumably with bad teeth, and disputed territory with their great rivals, the Upcans, which have spread widely from the Severn. Even as I watched, the Plastic Bag fish was punctured by the bottom-feeding Barbed Wire and, not far away, a lesser-coloured Paint Pot released its globules. Amongst this wealth of wildlife, I was fortunate enough to glimpse the ever-obsolescent Newspaper Bird, so I guessed that its mate, the filleted Fish-and-Chip Wrapper couldn't be far away. And there it was, by an array of Wallpaper Flowers which, much to the satisfaction of nature-lovers, brightens many a dull landscape.

Although lost in a reverie induced by all this natural beauty, I became aware of an alien ugliness. I became nauseated as I noticed and untidy spread of foxgloves, blue flowers flaming up stalks and burning bees into golden sparks. Unkempt ivy lounged ungeometrically over what had once been a clean white electric cooker. Its glossy enamel had been defiled by lichen and meadowsweet, each twirling hotplate struggling to warm itself in the sun. A chipped dinner plate, now dined off by vermin and wild cress, looked unlikely to survive, its fetching puce and bilious green transfer soon to be lost for ever. Deep melancholy afflicted me as a terrible truth struck me; if creeping and climbing plants proliferated unchecked, I might be witnessing the very last sheet of unvandalised corrugated iron.

Utterly scandalised at such carnage, completely nonplussed by this callousness so obviously not produced by anything remotely human, I must have allowed my sharp senses to relax. Such devastation was clearly the work of a monster with no vestige of aesthetic sensibility. I was so overawed, I didn't hear something creeping up stealthily behind me.

The roar blasted me off my feet. It uprooted trees. Chunks of Garreg Lwyd soared into the air and tumbled down the hillside. Recovering behind a boulder, I reached out and recovered my rifle.

Apart from cows whistling overhead, I could see nothing but swirling dust and leaves. I fired a barrage of shots, hoping to scare the monster away.

I must have succeeded; when the dust cleared, there was only sunlight. All I could hear was the buzz of insects. Hardly able to believe the closeness of my escape, I cautiously emerged from my hiding place and left the hideous lair.

What seemed like weeks later – my flask was empty – but must have been only hours, I began to recognise my surroundings. With indescribable relief, I sighted Camp One. As I staggered closer, I shouted to let Megan know I'd returned. She didn't reply. Then, beside the tent, I saw the abominable hoof-print.

I snatched at the flap. With a horror I can only describe as horrible, I was confronted by a horrific sight. Megan had gone. Apart from a thigh bone, its surface covered with teeth marks, only a few shreds of clothing bore witness to her awful fate. I shuddered and tried not to think of her screams as she was eaten alive. Her personal stereo remained, its unpalatable music, so to speak, serving for a dirge. Overcome by grief and exertion, I passed out.

What traumas I went through during the following days are consigned to my unconscious. I came round in a world which, unlike Brecon Beacons, was furnished with a soft bed. And a soft floor. And soft walls. I called out for a nurse and a ministering angel answered, his twenty-eight-inch biceps easing my straps.

But I have heartening news for you; the doctors say I shall soon be able to leave. I am my old, clear-sighted self again. And you'll be overjoyed to hear I've been poring over maps and planning the next expedition.

Difficult though it might be for you to believe, I am resolved once again to place my expertise at your disposal and risk my life in the cause of science. We must track down this monster which despoils areas of natural beauty and eats research assistants. I am, despite my terrifying ordeal, prepared to venture forth and, for my selflessness, I seek no reward. I ask for nothing but, God willing, success and a cheque for fifty thousand pounds. Upon receipt, I shall furnish myself once more with essential equipment, courage, fortitude, these wonderful blue tablets the nurse has given me and another undergraduate.

I am, esteemed Committee, and hope to remain,

Yours faithfully,

N.M.

Stocktaking

Shops that sell antiquarian books might get broken into occasionally, but twice at once seems excessive. At least, it does to me; I was one of the people breaking in.

Although I'm usually punctilious – and only someone punctilious would use that word – I didn't extend myself over this one. After all, I was after a single book, not the Alexandrian Library.

The shop stood in a quiet street in Bath. Amongst the honey-toned, Georgian facades, its brickwork looked a bit out of place, an orphan, like me, unsure of acceptance.

Its only alarm was a movement sensor. Normally, I'd research the make and model – if they weren't ones I knew – and knock up an electronic disabler. This time, as I was staying in a nearby hotel during the festival, all I did was set the thing off night after night. It wasn't difficult; I took a walking stick with me and poked it through the letter box.

Despite the music festival, the police weren't busy – in Bath, a couple of double-parking incidents is a crime wave – but they don't like their evening card game interrupted, especially for nothing. So the shop owner switched off his movement sensor and promised to get it repaired.

As I elbowed a small pane of glass on the door, I felt quite nostalgic; it was like being a wayward kid again, before the paraphernalia of keypads and pressure alarms and entrance codes. Headlight beams flashed around me as a car passed, but I was out of sight in the shop entrance. With my gloved hands, I picked out the pieces of window glass and let myself in.

I climbed a few stairs to the back room. The shop had once been a house, although it hadn't been lived in for ages. Upstairs, I knew from my one visit, were two more rooms of books. I closed the door to the back room. As it was windowless, I switched on the light.

Here they all were, the leather-bound volumes, the signed paperbacks, the hard-cover first editions. Clearly, to be kept in this room, you had to be special and valuable – individual. Each book, despite mass-production, had its own appeal and personality. I was about to locate the book I'd come for when I heard a creak on the stairs.

Some people – optimists – would tell themselves it was the wood shrinking, a drop in temperature causing the creak. Being a pessimist, I was certain it was a footfall.

I turned off the light. A few groping paces took me behind a table. The books on it, I recalled without merriment, described Victorian architecture. Particularly prisons.

Perhaps the shop had a cat. A very overweight cat. I like cats. They have all sorts of appealing characteristics and attributes – but they don't include turning a door knob, as this one was doing.

I heard the door inch open. A pause. Then I heard it close. I waited. Had the person gone? Maybe to the front door. If so, what about the broken pane?

I needn't have worried. Whoever it was wouldn't be inspecting the broken pane. I was sure of this. How? Because the intruder wasn't by the front door. The intruder was in the room with me.

You can strain to listen too much. I sensed rather than heard. An empiricist, I rely on my senses but, in extreme circumstances, maybe there's something else. I didn't have the time or inclination to pursue this; the light came on.

Crouching behind the table, all I could see was a stack of books. My nose was inches from H.G. Wells' 'The Invisible Man'.

'Can't find the book you're looking for?' enquired a voice.

I held my breath. I don't know why. A wish not to be seen or heard. A wish not to exist.

'Perhaps I can help you,' the voice said.

A female voice – that much registered. Thoughts whirled. A policewoman? The owner? A ghost?

Calming down, I began breathing again. Slowly, I stood up.

She was facing me. Being observant, I noticed she was between sixteen and seventy; her black outfit, complete with Balaclava mask, accounts for the margin for error. Her gloved hands hung by her side; I was grateful to see they were empty. Clearly, this wasn't the police or the owner with some weighty object for a weapon. It began to dawn on me she was a burglar. A bloody thief! And she couldn't have long given up reading 'Batman' or some other comic.

I'm not good at etiquette. I've always been a loner. But I suspected, in this situation, 'How do you do?' isn't appropriate. An affronted, 'What the hell are you doing here?' seemed possible, as though I was a legitimate occupant. But I'm a burglar, not a con man. Besides, it wouldn't fool *me*, never mind her.

'How do you do?' I said.

I can't be sure – she was covered head to toe – but she appeared to cringe.

'Hi,' I tried, unconvincingly.

'Do you come here often?' she intoned. Even I detected the scorn.

Twenty years I've been a burglar. I've never been caught, not even once. As far as criminal records and the police are concerned, I'm anonymous. I keep abreast of technological developments and I devise my own electronic gadgetry. Yet this, this shadow of a person, this renegade from 'The Beano', had the nerve to disdain me.

'We seem to be here for similar reasons,' I said. 'You'll find the comics in the front room.'

'Comics are considered art nowadays,' she replied haughtily. 'They're even used to disseminate philosophy.'

It was the word 'disseminate' that prodded me. Like 'punctilious', it raises the inner eyebrow.

I tried a new tack. 'This is clearly your first venture into this field. Your outfit does the opposite of concealing your amateurishness. How old are you?'

'Eighteen.'

I was shocked – not only by her age, but that she'd answered the question.

'How old do you have to be before you're a person?' she asked. There was a sudden weariness in her voice, but she soon reasserted herself. 'I need to find out who I am – or *if* I am.'

There are times – in a cosy pub, say – when you know it's time to go. Someone starts confiding in you and, pretty quickly, the raging snowstorm outside seems preferable.

'As we're here on similar missions,' I said, 'let's make our selections and go our separate ways.'

'Which book were you looking for?' she asked.

A number of titles flashed through my head. 'Farewell, My Lovely' was a strong contender.

I glanced at her outfit again. She'd turned a fraction and, now, on her belt, I could see a phone in a pouch.

'I don't believe it!' I gasped. 'You've come here – with a phone! You're expecting a friend to call? – to have a chat?' I took a deep breath and forced myself to calm down. 'How did you get in? An upstairs window?'

'The roof. I clambered across gables and removed a few slates.'

Just like that. She seemed so casual. When I was a youngster on my first solo job, I was tense. She was a mystery.

Until she said, 'I'm a philosophy student. At Bath University.'

Short of giving me her telephone number, her cover, black and all-encompassing though it was, couldn't have been more superfluous.

'It was a first edition of Hume's 'A Treatise of Human Nature', I said. 'The book I was looking for.'

'You study philosophy?' she asked, as though the idea was ludicrous.

Which, I admit, it was. To a certain extent. 'No,' I replied. 'I steal to order. One of my clients wants it.' And then I stopped, alarmed I'd volunteered so much.

'Don't let me hinder you.'

She didn't look as though she'd hinder me. She looked unconcerned. As I couldn't see her facial expression, I visualised the one I wanted.

I turned to the bookshelves and searched. Best to get the job done and be on my way. But the book didn't appear to be there.

'Can't you find it?'

I couldn't. It wasn't where I saw it when I'd visited. Surely it hadn't been sold in the past few days? Just my luck.

'Hume's not here,' I complained.

'Appropriate then.'

'Meaning?'

'He couldn't find himself,' she said. 'Or *any* self. Only a sequence of perceptions – the ideas and memories looked at. Not the looker.'

The raging snowstorm outside, had there been one, became positively inviting. I've always thought it's a mistake to teach philosophy to kids: first, because it can be depressing and, second, because it's bollocks. I mean, philosophy claims to employ logic, yet comes up with multiple, contradictory answers.

'Surely,' I said, 'students aren't so hard up they have to steal books?'

'I'm not here to steal books.'

'No?' I tried to look quizzical. 'My logic might not be as developed as yours, but this is a book shop and you've broken into it; ergo, you're here to steal books. Or have I missed some quantum leap in thinking?'

'I was a Buddhist.'

Evidently I had. I was reasonably bright at school. I learned grammar and my multiplication tables – all right, they're not exactly predicate calculus, but I managed. So I didn't like being confused by an angst-ridden teenager. She was like something out of a thought experiment.

'Anyway,' she added helpfully, 'I don't care much about owning things or coveting them.'

'I see,' I said, light dawning. Then it clouded over again. 'So you broke in here to…? Burn joss sticks? Meditate on the Eightfold Path?'

'Hardly' she scoffed. 'That would be silly.'

'God forbid.'

'No,' she said as she moved towards a corner. 'I'm here to break into the safe.'

I couldn't help staring. I hadn't realised – and I don't like admitting this – that there *was* a safe. She moved a couple of piles of books and there it was: an old Chubb combination.

A host of questions raised their hands, like an overcrowded class of schoolchildren.

'If you don't care about owning things…' was the first and most insistent. It couldn't even wait for a question mark.

'I'm hardly going to pillage the place,' she replied.

Before I had time to think, my second question found voice. 'How can a Buddhist decide to do such a thing? In fact, how can a Buddhist decide to do *anything*? If you don't see yourself as a single ego, merely as a walking bundle theory, who's in charge?'

She turned to look at me. 'So you *have* read philosophy.'

'Hell no. I'd rather do cryptic crosswords, or count raindrops, or have my feet boiled in oil. All I'm saying is that perceptions, whether yours or Hume's, can't make decisions.'

'You understand,' she sighed. There was relief in her voice. 'I thought I was the only one – which, for a Buddhist, is about as near to blasphemy as you can get.'

'You're losing your conviction?' I asked, trying not to look at my watch.

She faced me, then took off her Balaclava. As she shook her hair loose, I saw a fresh-faced girl with pale skin.

'I don't know why I chose a philosophy course,' she said. 'Or any course, come to that. I'm not very suited to engaging with things.'

'Blowing safes doesn't count?'

'I'm not going to blow it,' she smiled. 'Of course not.'

I was relieved to hear it. For me, the Chubb wouldn't be much of a challenge, if I'd had my equipment with me.

'You're not a happy person, are you?' she asked, pity softening her voice.

The snowstorm outside turned into a hurricane. I imagined whole trees whistling past and longed to be amongst them.

'Is it due to your upbringing?'

'I was an orphan,' I replied. Sometimes, words just rush out before I give them permission. 'The truth is' – well, I'd started, so what the hell – 'I feel as though I've never really had any choice.'

'How did you become a burglar?'

'My foster Father taught me,' I said. 'I suppose everything's cause and effect.'

'Twaddle!' She looked dismissive. 'Determinism's just an excuse.'

'Everything that happens has to be dependent on something that caused it,' I said.

'You really believe that?'

'Of course. Otherwise the world wouldn't operate the way it does. Events would be random.'

She looked back to the safe. 'You told me there must be something that views ideas and perceptions. It's what's worried me for some time. Now,' she added, turning away, 'I've got a safe to open.'

'What method are you going to use?' I asked, doubt in my voice. Even so, I moved forward for a better view. 'Stethoscope? Drill?'

'This outfit's tight-fitting,' she replied. 'Do you see a concealed stethoscope or drill?'

I let my eyes wander over her body. They took their time. Apart from the phone, they didn't, among the bumps and curves, detect anything like a stethoscope or drill. They checked again anyway.

She knelt down, flexed her fingers, closed her eyes, opened them, took a deep breath, then turned the knob back and forth.

The safe clicked open.

'That's amazing,' I gasped. 'How did you do it? Some kind of Zen concentration?'

'Not really,' she said. 'I knew the number.'

That's the trouble with mysticism; it always turns out a deception – usually *self*-deception. We want to believe in it, of course, but that's our ancient, Jungian self desperate to escape reality.

'My uncle owns this place,' she said as she pulled open the safe door. 'It wasn't difficult to find out the combination.'

I'm used to disillusion. Yet, somehow, it still manages to surprise me. Still, if the safe held cash, there might be compensation.

'If you were able to get the combination,' I said, 'why couldn't you get the front door key?'

Taking papers out of the safe, she said, 'It was the movement sensor; I didn't know how to disable it. Thanks for doing it for me.'

'My pleasure,' I said, not quite gritting my teeth. She sorted through papers and brown envelopes.

'It began to go off each night,' she continued. 'On the third night, I was watching.'

I was evidently taking this job too casually. I'd even been thinking of shoplifting the Hume book – until I saw the size of it. But what she was saying didn't make complete sense.

She continued to inspect the safe's contents. Still no money.

'The break-in must be attributed to *you*,' she said.

'I see.'

'You, as in unknown professional burglar,' she added.

'You're not as clever as you think,' I said. 'The police will find two places of entry; the roof and the door.'

'Got it!' she exclaimed and pulled out the contents of a large brown envelope. I frowned. All I could see were photocopies of official-looking documents.

'Two places of entry?' She glanced at me. 'You're rather gullible, aren't you?'

I'm not known as a violent person. I'm seldom in fights and I certainly haven't murdered anyone. Yet.

'If I'd come in through the roof,' she continued, 'I'd have made enough noise to wake concertgoers in the Guildhall. And I'd be covered in dirt and cobwebs, wouldn't I?'

So what was she doing? Acting out some private drama? A Buddhist Batwoman? A philosophising fantasist?

'Right,' she said, standing up. 'I've got what I came for.'

But that didn't make sense either. She'd looked at the contents of the large brown envelope – and replaced it intact in the safe.

I crouched and rummaged. There was no money – not even a petty-cash box. Again, I couldn't decide which question to ask first.

'Let me explain,' she said, as though reading my mind. 'I followed you in.'

From a pocket, she produced a key and waggled it. I wasn't feeling at my sharpest, but even I worked out it fitted the front door.

'All right,' I said, 'I'm your fall guy. But what evidence is there that I exist? As far as anyone can tell, you're the only…'

My voice trailed off. Lights in my head were beginning to come on – almost literally.

'When the headlights flashed across the doorway…' I pondered out loud. 'That was when…' I glanced at the phone on her belt. 'You took a photo of me, didn't you?'

Her grin confirmed it. I was doing well; I'd managed to link two thoughts. For me, at the moment, that was the equivalent of producing the theory of relativity.

'Don't worry,' she said. 'It won't be clear enough to identify you.'

'But clear enough to clear *you*,' I said. 'How do you know I won't take your phone and destroy it?'

'Because I sent the photo straight to my computer.'

'Fair enough.'

'If I need to produce the photo,' she added, 'I'll do it anonymously. I'm good at being anonymous. In fact, that's what this is all about.'

'It is?' I tried to make it sound less than a question. I didn't succeed.

'Have you heard of Theseus' ship?' she asked.

As a matter of fact, I had, but felt this wasn't really the time or place to discuss it.

'Aren't you worried the police might turn up?' I asked.

'Not a lot. They seldom drive down this street. Besides, I covered your broken pane with an ad' for Morris dancing.'

'You did *what*?' I exclaimed.

'You don't approve?'

'Is there no tactic you won't stoop to? *Morris* dancing?'

She ignored that and re-boarded Theseus' ship.

'The ship was preserved,' she said, 'but, over time, every plank and beam rotted and had to be replaced. Could it still be called Theseus' ship?'

'You're forgetting your ova,' I said.

For a change, it was she who was puzzled.

'All the cells of your body are replaced,' I said, 'except your ova and lens. As for whoever dreamt up the Theseus metaphor, well, the windows of his soul need glasses.'

'That doesn't work,' she complained.

'Exactly. Nor do so many philosophical metaphors. The brain cells that replace dead cells clearly inherit a lot more than planks that replace planks.'

She remained silent for a moment, then seemed to make a decision.

'That,' she said, a wave of one hand indicating the safe, 'is to do with relationships.'

'I see...' I said slowly, none the wiser.

'My uncle. He's a bastard.'

'There are other ways to get at him,' I said.

'I mean his parents weren't married.'

'I thought,' I said with a smile, 'you meant he's a swine.'

'That too.'

I'm glad I'm a burglar. It's a simple life. All right, you need to keep up with technology, but you know where you are. And who you are. It doesn't have to get complicated. There's the moral side to deal with, of course, but how often do you meet people who can't justify their behaviour?

'I felt I was a nobody,' she continued. 'Maybe that's why Buddhism seemed natural to me. But I've become more individual, less placid, and I resent its teachings more and more.'

'So pick another belief. As a philosophy student, you've plenty to choose from.'

'I found out I was adopted,' she continued. 'But it was unofficial. My adoptive parents refuse to tell me more and I drew a blank with the official agencies.'

I tried to work out what this had to do with becoming Cat Woman and robbing a shop. Fortunately, she got to that bit next.

'Uncle Jack, who owns this shop, told me he knows all the family history. That's because his hobby, apart from something I won't mention, is genealogy. I suppose it's because his Mother wasn't married. Anyway, he's kept my parentage to himself and used it as a psychological weapon.'

At last, it became clear.

'That envelope you looked in,' I said. 'Genealogy?'

'I found copies of birth and marriage certificates.'

'In that case, why haven't you made photocopies?' I asked. 'There's a copier in the front of the shop.'

She smiled. 'I'm not as bright as the average undergraduate.'

'You seem to do all right,' I said with restraint.

'That's not because I'm especially bright; it's because I have a very retentive memory.'

'Just glancing at those documents was enough?'

'I've got all I need to know,' she said. 'I'll write it out later. I need a sense of self, whether it's a fiction or not.'

'Yet you don't think you're a product of the past?' I said, closing the safe.

'Of course I am. But that's not the same as determinism. Do you really think that every word and every comma in all these,' – she indicated the shelves of books – 'was pre-ordained in the Big Bang?'

I could see where this was leading. It was accept-you're-responsible time again.

'In quantum theory,' I replied, 'cause and effect isn't the whole story.' Well, I had to try.

'As though randomness would be any better,' she scoffed. 'The random functioning of your brain would be a wonderful excuse, wouldn't it?'

'Look, I don't need all this! I only came to nick a book!'

'Hume's book.'

'Sod it, he won't mind!' I said. 'He'd be pleased.'

'He didn't find a self that views perceptions,' she said, 'but the fact that we can decide which perceptions to view indicates we have choice.'

I made for the door and reached for the light switch.

'Wait, she said, placing a hand on my arm. 'You might be a product of your past, but you have a choice.'

'Which is also the product of the past,' I said.

'Yes, the possibility of choice, not the choice made. Influences may be great; they're not insurmountable.'

'The choice I'm making at the moment,' I said, 'is to get out of here. We haven't taken anything, but one of us isn't leaving empty-handed.'

'I'm not a thief,' she said hastily, 'and I wouldn't be an accomplice to one…'

She obviously hadn't finished, so I waited.

'…but it wouldn't be immoral if I mentioned that Uncle Jack's in the middle of a re-organisation. Besides, as I said, he's a bastard!'

Taking the hint, and not wishing her new-born, innocent self to be sullied, I looked towards the piles of books. And, for the first time, noticed a box of labels next to a pair of scissors. Of course! The piles of books weren't due to untidiness or lack of space; Uncle Jack was re-arranging his stock.

I must be slowing down or growing complacent, I thought.

A few strides took me to an unfilled shelf. And there, next to other antiquarian volumes, was Hume.

'Hello, old chap,' I said warmly. 'He who was lost has been found.'

I took down the book and, back by the door, turned off the light. We passed through to the front of the shop.

I automatically whispered. 'You're going out dressed like that? It's a miracle you weren't arrested on the way here.'

'It's only a miracle,' she replied, picking up what was clearly her coat, 'if, as Hume says, it's more likely than being a false report.'

I was miffed. I'd got what I came for, but it hadn't been a good night.

She put on her coat and looked anonymous again. I hoped her full-dress adventure had made her feel better about herself. Looking out through the shop windows, I carefully checked the street was clear.

There were things we could have said on parting. One of them wasn't, 'What's your name?' I'm not the most trusting of souls and this encounter had done nothing to convert me. As we stepped into the street, we made eye-contact, then walked in opposite directions.

On my way to the hotel, I began to think about things. There was a lot to consider. And maybe a choice to be made.

Some other day.

About the Author

Neal Mason has had a number of poetry collections published, including books by Peterloo Poets, the University of Salzburg Press and Holland Park Press and a novel is now available on Amazon. He has done well in many competitions, including winning the Phoenix International Play Competition on two consecutive years. He taught courses for the University of Wales, WEA etc. and was Writer in Residence for six months in a Welsh valley. He was selected for a masterclass at the Hay-on-Wye Festival and advised the Arts Council's Grants to Publishers Panel. He runs the soundwork-uk.co.uk website. Incongruously, he was an international athlete when young and, at the time of writing, holds the European Masters Record for the pole vault in his age group.

Previous Publications by Neal Mason

Poetry Preview 2
(Peterloo Poets 1990)

Excavations
(Peterloo Poets 1991)

Leading the Guidebook Astray
(University of Salzburg Press 1995)

The Past is a Dangerous Driver
(Holland Park Press 2022)

Love Can Wait
(Michael Terence Publishing 2024)

A Wisp of Brute Force
(Michael Terence Publishing 2024)

*Available worldwide from Amazon
and all good bookstores*

———————————

Michael Terence
Publishing

www.mtp.agency

www.facebook.com/mtp.agency

@mtp_agency

Milton Keynes UK
Ingram Content Group UK Ltd.
UKHW041959291124
451915UK00004B/322

9 781800 949089